Flesh and Blood

Edited by Sally Alexander and Piers Blaikie

Contributors:

Sally Alexander, Piers Blaikie, Mags Chalcraft, Angela Drake,
Martin Drummond, Elspeth Latimer, Jenny Morris,
Anne Olerenshaw, Sheila Preston, Keith Rose,
Jack Rosenthal, Rosemary Smith, Sultan Walpole

GATEHOUSE PRESS LTD

Published by
Gatehouse Press Limited
Bridge House, Bridge Street
Halesworth, Suffolk IP19 8AQ
www.gatehousepress.com

First Published in Great Britain by
Gatehouse Press Limited 2010

The right of Sally Alexander and Piers Blaikie to be identified as
the editors of this work has been asserted by them in accordance
with Section 77 of the Copyright, Designs and Patent Act 1988.

ISBN 978-0-9562083-9-2

Cover design by Lucien Francis

Printed in Great Britain by the MPG Books Group,
Bodmin and King's Lynn

Contents

Foreword

Flesh and Blood – butcher's block, Shylock's slip, murder and mayhem, or family feeling – *Flesh and Blood* gathers all into a kaleidoscope of life – and death. Turn the page, change the scene. It is the living matter of which we are each composed and that which, when disturbed, can bring us to a gory end. But beyond that, flesh and blood is the very stuff which unites and links us as living creatures. In an age of science, we are able to identify familiar links through a drop of blood and trace a person's history through a shard of bone. It is in the complexities of family relations, those who share their flesh and blood, that many of our writers have found inspiration. *Flesh and Blood* tells of the workings of people that cannot be captured by science – their love and hate; their confusion and affection; their passions and mistrusts. Bound together by flesh and blood, these poems and stories say something about what it means to be human.

We open with two poems: 'Snow Cover' and 'One Flesh, One Blood', which traverse the two major themes family and death mourning the loss of loved ones, those who shared their flesh and blood. Death rather than loss takes a more central role in other stories. In meticulous detail a death is planned, but can the planners face the ever-so-natural consequence? 'Will There Be Much Blood?' is a comic and very possible and frightening account of setting up a contract murder

We meet regret and guilt in 'The Bridge', where a woman, having escaped a suicide pact as a teenager, finds redemption in death. Another character facing his end is found in 'Tweet, Tweet'. This time, he is not alone, as he tells his story of flesh and blood to an unlikely and unseen confidant - and nemesis? 'Frank Solomon' is an old man living in a tied cottage in rural Norfolk, but even this hardy character has his breaking point. With a lighter touch comes 'Blood Type'. A Quentin Crisp-like character befriends a young girl in a library and attempts to discover the cause of her unhappiness. It seems that not flesh, but blood will solve this story.

'The Bonds That Bind' tells of a woman who agrees to become a surrogate mother for her sister and they work through their rivalrous history. Will she be able to give up the babies, or break her sister's heart? For more siblings' relationships we travel to the west coast of

Ireland for 'The Whale', which tells of a young boy remembering his sister's drowning and his possible responsibility for it.

Parental relationships are explored in a number of stories. In 'The Slipper', a long stretch of history is told at a breathless and brutal pace. Cinderella and the wicked stepmother have never appeared so different. In 'Homecoming', a nineteenth-century Scot returns 'home' to India and is met by feverish visions of a flesh and blood child he never knew he wanted. The estranged parent is also taken as a key figure in 'Not Much to Tell', where a woman searches for her biological father, though there is little hope that 'Pa' could live up to expectation. In 'Loss', we meet a father who distances himself from his son when he disapproves of his son's choice of wife. Will he ever be able to mend the bridges that he has broken? Resolution of a sort is found in 'Inheritance', which recalls the history of a mother forced to place her son in the care system, but the surprising encounters at the reading of her will offer answers he did not even know he was searching for.

Turn the page, change the scene. Our stories and poems do the rest.

Sally Alexander
Piers Blaikie

Snow Cover
Angela Drake

I drove north in a snowstorm, the sky full.
The onslaught was silent, soft, relentless.
No warmth to melt the splinter in the soul.

I passed right by the place. In thick darkness,
with cover of snow, nothing could be seen.
No tracks, no twisted metal, blood or flesh,

no shattered bone or broken tree. All clean.
As though no-one had died. As though you might
come back. As though it had all been a dream.

The car stalled. I thought I saw you then, light
streaming through you, against the night. I saw
your face and body shining silver white.

But you were gone. From the east, ice winds tore
through vast snow clouds. Over black sea the sun
streaked blood red. The hard snows would not yet thaw.

I will go on. It cannot be undone,
till bread and wine and flesh and blood are one.

One Flesh, One Blood
Angela Drake

It's been too long
since I walked through bluebell woods holding your hand,
picnicked with you on summer beaches,
built sandcastles at the water's edge.

I watch you,
peaceful for now in a hospital bed,
connected, by a thread of vein,
to monitors on this side of Life.

Outside, sleet streaks white across a lowering sky,
cars make their way home.

I walk endless corridors,
pathways between waking and sleeping, shadow and light,
etched in your face.

Your pain,
my pain.

Fragments of laughter return,
your voice calling, singing,
quick footsteps dancing, arms lifting me,
sun in your blue eyes smiling,
perfume, as you kiss me goodnight.

One flesh,
one blood.

The same when you breathed me to life,
mother to daughter.
Now lips, eyes, skin
pale and fade.

You lie still.
Life hovers, suspended on your faltering breath.

I hold your hand,
your fingers through my fingers,
daughter to mother.
Stand at the water's edge,

watch, until night comes,
as it must,
and the tides flood in to gather you
to that Greater mother,
to that unfathomable Light.

Will There Be Much Blood?
Keith Rose

August 2012. Room 202 in the Holiday Inn, Indianapolis

Mr Thackeray?

Yes?

I'm from the Book Depository.

OK. Come in. You are punctual. I like that.

Thank you. I'm glad to meet you, sir.

You know I do not like this. I do not like to meet. And, please…
do not call me sir.

*OK. I wanted to let you know that we have just completed the second
transfer.*

I know this already. I was checking on my laptop. I explained. I
don't move forward without the next instalment. I have it now. So I
can proceed.

You're ready?

I am nearly ready. Certain things must be left until the final
hours.

Are you confident, Mr Thackeray?

Listen. This is not a good question. If you want to hire somebody
else…

*No, we're happy. Don't get rattled. But success now is key. It's our last
chance. We'll need time to introduce the new candidate. People don't like
surprises in this election game, Thackeray.*

I do not like surprises. It is going according to the plan.

I'm glad to hear that. To hear it straight from the guy himself.

Good.

But you don't look like…

I don't look like what?

Your name. Your voice. Not what I expected.

You should not expect anything. Except the result.

*Yeah, the result. The result's the important thing. And you? You'll
disappear? Vanish into thin air…?*

Yes. That is the deal.

The distraction of the search, you see. It'll be helpful.

Will it?

4

If they catch you straight away, it would be…. very messy.

Yes. For me, as well as for you.

Of course. Not pleasant for you. Er, will you excuse me if I use the bathroom?

It is there.

Thanks… I want you to know, Thackeray – and you might think it's odd to tell you this when I'm having a piss – but I want you to know that I'm in this because I'm a patriot.

You're a patriot.

Ah, that's better… Yeah, I'm a patriot. All of us are patriots. We love our country.

You love your country.

Do you love your country, Mr Thackeray?

Yes, I love my country.

But it's not this country. You're not an American?

Is this relevant to the job here?

Yeah, for me, it is relevant. Mighty relevant. What the hell's that silver thing on the table?

My samovar.

Your what?

My samovar. I drink tea when I am working.

You drink tea.

It helps me to focus.

*Where **are** you from, Thackeray?*

Look, I have a job here. Is this a second interview?

No, no. It's OK. I'm just… just interested.

I was born in Krasnoyarsk.

Which I guess is not in the U.S.

No, not in the U.S.

I see. And where did you learn your… trade?

This is why I do not like to meet. No more questions. No more.

OK. We'll keep it professional. We just need a good clean job… Will there be… er… much blood?

Oh, do not worry. There will be no blood. I am experienced. Unless perhaps your friend from Alaska has a heart. And arteries. And all the other usual body parts. What! Are you dumb? Of course there will be blood! That is what happens when you shoot somebody. Perhaps if you add another million dollars to the third instalment, we can arrange to have no blood…

I'm sorry. Forget I mentioned that. I'm expecting too much. I only asked because…. because the American people will find the sight of blood in the convention hall very, very upsetting.

5

And you must not upset your beloved American people!

Now, go easy, Thackeray. I explained. We are doing this because I sincerely believe we are facing a crisis here. A monumental crisis. That candidate is a loose cannon. She would be a disaster, I say a disaster for our country, our economy, our place in the world. Our party needs to replace her. But we don't want to cause unnecessary distress.

So my job is to cause necessary distress.

I should not have brought this up.

No.

Well… er… I'm glad you say you're ready.

I am ready.

And for your sake, I hope the exit is easy.

Yes.

It's only… er… I never met anybody doing a job like this. You might say it's an unusual calling.

Not where I come from.

And 'Thackeray.' What kind of name is that?

My father liked reading.

Reading?

He was English teacher. He liked British novels. Especially nineteenth-century.

And he christened you Thackeray?

No. That is my name for this job.

I see.

Good.

And you like your work?

You like **your** work?

Yeah. No. Sometimes there are things I don't like. But I do it.

We understand each other.

No, I don't think we do. To begin with, you're not an American.

And you think I do not understand your famous 'liberty'?

Not in the way we do.

No, not in the way you do. I was a child of the Soviet. I hated the Soviet. But my father, he could borrow books by Thackeray from the library. And I could walk to bakery opposite our apartment. Even when it was minus 50 degrees. I could get warm bread for my father. And it was so cold the bread froze to my hands as I walked back to my home. But we had hot soup on the stove. And my father read us chapters from William Makepeace Thackeray. It was my community. It was my kind of liberty.

But you didn't stay.

Now everything in Krasnoyarsk, it stinks. So I left. I got a job and then I left. And here I am…. Do you have any further instructions?

Minus 50 degrees.

Minus 50 degrees.

No wonder you're so cool.

It is my job to be cool. Do you have further instructions?

Yeah, there's a lot that stinks in this country. Your job is to start the cleanup. Just to start it. We'll finish the job. But you can start it. You can get those goddam rimless spectacles off our TV screens.

You do not like her, do you?

It is not a question of what I like or who I like. It's a matter of saving the future. Of taking control of things. Your part is to fire the starting pistol on the whole process.

I shall fire the starting pistol.

For Chrissake, you know what I mean.

Oh, yes, I know what you mean.

Is that it? On the bed, in that black case?

Look, I do not know your name. I do not wish to know your name. But there have been too many questions, mister. Thank you for the instalment. But now you must trust me.

Trust you?

Yes. In your business schools they call it delegation.

Hey, Thackeray, don't talk to me about delegation.

No?

Why d'you think I am here? You imagine the party said: 'Oh, as long as you're passing the Holiday Inn, do drop in on Thackeray. He's a regular guy. Give him our best wishes.' Eh?

The party chose one candidate. Now some of you in the party want another.

Some of us know how to take the long-term view.

My job is to take the short-term view. I even have special viewfinder to help me. Would you like to see it? And then… perhaps you will depart, a happy man.

OK, OK. My God, this is a bad business.

Here. One of my rifle sights. A tool of my trade. Do not touch. You have no gloves... And in this case here, there is another… for night-time. If you switch the lights off at your convention. You like to do things like that. Have you seen enough? Do you want to see the rifle? It's gas-operated. Semi-automatic. Do you know about rifles? I can disassemble in less than three minutes, and when…

I get your point, Thackeray. I get your point.

I said, I am ready.

I'll report back.

And tell them I am not interested in your candidate. I do not care what she says. I do not care if you hate her. I do not care about her glasses. I just do my job.

You do your job. OK.

OK.

I'll let them know.

You tell your patriotic friends.

I will.

And the third instalment. If it does not arrive, tell them I shall return. I do not want to come back, because everything will be a mess. It always is. But tell them in the Book Depository that I can return. Maybe to your next convention.

The third instalment will be fine. Don't you worry, Thackeray. And it won't be a mess. At last we'll have some order. It is for the greater good.

It's fine to hear some proper Soviet thinking.

What d'you mean?

Would you like to drink some of my tea before you leave?

No. I believe I've finished here.

OK. Then I can begin.

That's right, my friend, you can begin. You've got the schedule. We'll expect it tomorrow.

Tomorrow.

Tomorrow, the beginning of stability. Goodbye, Mr Thackeray.

Goodbye, Mr Patriot.

The Bridge
Mags Chalcraft

Dear Jules,
I wanted you to know. At last. I've done it.
Love,
Nikki xxx

I've taken the pills. Ten of the maximum strength Ibuprofen and all of the Paracetamol. I've taken the Nurofen too, that the woman in the white coat at the chemist gave me. I asked for something for period pains. She gave me a funny look. She thought I was too old for that.

So I've swallowed them all, one after the other. No mistakes this time. They look so clean and innocent, cradled in their little silver beds. So smooth and white. It's easily done.

Now I'm sitting on the couch, waiting. I reckon it's a nicer way to die. Less fuss. No messing about with blades, or ropes. No blood. No bath tub filled with reddening water.

I used to think it might work out. There were times I felt happy. When I first met Rory. Playing pool at The George. Sitting on the back steps with him, smoking fags. As if no one had ever played pool or smoked before. And the day Darren was born. Holding him in the hospital bed. Holding the wrapped bundle until my shoulders screamed; and then holding him some more. Refusing to let go.

Sometimes I thought it might turn out all right, after all. But let's be honest. That was a long time ago. I've made a mess of it. I was given a chance. And I screwed it up.

The lights are off and the room is grey. The curtains are shut.

I've left a note for her. In the end I didn't know what to say. Silly, because I've written and rewritten it, over the years. It's not as if she'll ever read it. She's been gone a long time.

A faint buzzing is beginning at the back of my head. I think I'll lie down. I'm feeling cold, but a slow warmth is making its way into my body, from the toes upwards.

I am back at the bridge. I can feel the rush of air in my ears and the exhilaration of height; of so much open space around us. I see her red scarf whipping off and the straight line she describes; not a tumbling acrobatic fall, but a leaden peregrine dive. Then she is a body. A doll on the rock below.

It was a cold day. I was wearing one glove. I had chilblains on my fingers, as usual. A Tuesday morning, but we weren't wearing school uniform. I had on my favourite jeans and Jules was wearing a long skirt with purple tassels.

As we walked to the bridge we talked. One or two cars passed. If you knew, I thought, looking at the drivers' faces. You'd stop right now and park your cars at funny angles and run up to us.

'Don't do this!' you'd shout.

But we wouldn't have listened. We were untouchable. We had our pact. Jules and Nik.

We talked about Mr Hodgeson. About what he would say when we were found. About what they would all say, back at Laurel Gates. I wished I could be there to see their faces, afterwards. To see who would be sad at the funeral. Standing in the church; or kneeling, hands pressed to their foreheads. And the newspaper reports. Blurred photographs of the two of us. Younger, smiling, with school ties and braces on our teeth. Photographs of dead girls. Cheerful, frozen in a time before. People would look at them and see a shadow, as if death was already written in the eyes.

Jules said some of them wouldn't give a toss. I laughed. She was always full of energy. She was full of inspiration. Jules had bright eyes.

They are still bright, I see, as she leans on the worktop. She has appeared in my kitchen, although I'm not really feeling up to visitors. It must be the pills, making me feel like this. No way now of telling what's real.

I try to tell her she's interrupting.

'It's not a good time, Juliet. I am trying to die.'

But she ignores that. She asks me if I'd like a cup of tea. Making herself at home. Taking over already. Striding to put the kettle on. Long legs in jeans; perfect hair.

She doesn't mention the bridge. Doesn't ask why I let her down. Why I chickened out.

I am still lying on the couch. I'm not sure where my hands and feet are; they have floated off somewhere.

She tells me she's an actress now. The jump didn't kill her, she explains. She decided not to come back to the home after it happened.

She wanted to make a new life for herself. You should have told me, I say. Thirty-five years is a long time. She comes through and sits next to me. Near the edge so she won't touch me under my blanket. She looks like she uses one of those expensive face creams. No wrinkles at all. She's looking around the room, taking in the mess. The stack of washing up in the sink, the piles of clothes, the damp feel of everything.

'So, Nik,' she says. 'Did you have kids?'

'Yes,' I answer. 'Two boys.'

I think of the two of them when they were small. Their skinny bodies, with bits sticking out. Shoulders, knees, elbows. White bones under blue skin.

'I was lucky,' she says. 'I got one of each.'

'Lovely,' I say.

'You blink and they're grown up.'

I blink. My eyes take longer to open again than they should. I'm not sure what I've missed. She is saying: 'At least they're happy. That's the main thing.'

She hasn't asked the question but I'm answering anyway.

'Oh, you know. This and that. Not sure what Darren's up to these days. He never got straight after his dad left. And Grady. Well. He's a law unto himself.' I try to smile. A strange, cracked thing that makes my top lip stretch over my teeth.

She doesn't answer, so I say, 'It must be great, Jules, working in telly.'

'When I think how far I've come. People find it hard to believe, when they hear about my background. And there's Steve of course.'

Her eyes are turned upwards and to the side. She's smiling a dreamy smile. Not focusing on the ceiling where it meets the wall, with its patina of dust, but watching a film inside her head. The cartoon strip of her life, being played out along the cornice. Lying here, going hot and cold, I wonder at my own imagination. Inventing stories for ghosts. But then I've always, since that day, been painting this picture. Building it up, layer by glossy layer.

'He's always stood by me,' Jules is saying. 'Didn't mind about Laurel Gates, about any of it. He just loves me for what I am. He's a good man. There you go, Nik. You see. They really do exist!'

She laughs. I adjust my focus from the faded part of the curtains to her face.

'Like fuck they do,' I say.

I don't think she has heard me.

'We live in Strawberry Fields,' she goes on. 'The new development

11

on the other side of town? It's Queen Anne. Whatever that is.' She laughs again. I think of the path through my own estate, lined with cans and glass and the brown stalks of weeds. The dark hallways, condoms on the floor. Walls decorated with penises.

She is looking at the white lines that criss-cross my lower arms, like a lattice of threadworms. She won't ask me how I got them. She'll be gone soon, back to Strawberry Fields. She stands up and when she speaks again her voice is shrill.

'What about you, Nik? What have you done with your life? All those years of life you got?'

I can't look her in the eye.

'It wasn't my fault, Jules,' I say. 'I'm not as brave as you.' I gesture round the room. 'I'm sorry.'

But it's all right now. I'm making it up to her. I tell her this. I tell her I'm going back to the bridge. This time I'll jump. I've already jumped, in a way. I've done it, Jules.

But she is gone. Leaving only the still air. It's as if she was never there at all.

Mr Hodgeson is my next visitor. The old manager from Laurel Gates. He hasn't aged, although he must be ancient by now. Why him? I wonder. I tell him I'm in a hurry. Jules is waiting for me at the bridge. I need to be off. He looks into my face.

'But you're on the kitchen floor,' he says. 'And your friend Juliet passed away a long time ago. As you well know.'

He was never one to mince his words.

'You didn't make much of yourself, Nicola. You should have tried harder. You were the lucky one.'

Sanctimonious git.

'You could've stopped us,' I say. 'We were just kids.'

He thinks for a moment. 'You weren't badly treated. Why did you do it?'

I realise he's here because we both want to know. Whether it was his fault. His black-and-white mind can only see it in terms of a case to be answered. Dotted lines chasing their tails around a piece of paper.

I don't expect him to understand what it feels like not to be special to anyone. To be nobody's little girl.

'You'll see,' I say quietly. 'It'll be different now that I'm dead. People will start to notice me.'

'You're not dead yet.'

Nice one, Hodge. Well observed.

He leans down and takes me by the shoulder. 'Who do you think I am? D'you think I'm God?'

I don't answer. I have gone back inside my head. Parts of the room are retreating into blackness. I am fading.

'Come back Nicola!' he shouts, in his bossing-about voice. 'Come back here!'

A spiral of sounds that bounce off me and fly about the room, becoming tinier and paler until they are sucked out of the window and into the open air.

I take the back road to the bridge. It all looks the same, just as I remember it. I can see her there, waiting for me. Jules at sixteen. Long plait down her back. I fall into step beside her. In her shadow again. She is talking, running rings of words round me, as always.

Now we are standing at the edge, arms bent back to hold on to the rail, shoulders pointed forwards. Like fledglings about to take our first flight from the nest. Hold hands, she commands. Her white hand grips mine, the one without a glove. Now the moment of stillness is here, just as I remember it. We are not talking anymore. We are each going through our own thoughts. This is where we have to separate, where we have to find our own reasons for launching into blank air.

This is the moment I have been afraid of all along. One step and my hair will fly upwards. Like a sky diver.

Like before, I slip my hand out of hers. I have small hands, they can betray easily. But this time it is different. Before she has time to draw breath, I launch, pouring myself out like water over the lip of a jug. She is left there, watching from the bridge. She will see me, reaching the ground impossibly quickly. Then it will be my turn to be the doll on the rock.

I feel the impact, a thudding in my chest that grows stronger.

The rock is warm, as if the sun has been shining on it all day. The warmth flows into my body.

You will never do it now, Jules. Without me. Without the exciting taste of our shared secret. You won't be able to go through with it.

Soon you will run back to Laurel Gates, shaking and stopping on the way to vomit at the foot of a wall. Mr Hodgeson will come out of his office in the lobby.

'Where have you been?' he'll ask. 'Where is Nicola? Why aren't you at school?'

'She jumped off the bridge,' you'll say. 'I couldn't stop her.' Your stomach will heave with the lie.

Then you'll have to face the questions. The sudden interest of policemen and policewomen. The social workers; the long, fidgeting silences in the counsellor's room. The journalists and the black eyes of the cameras.

But it will be different for you. You will enjoy your role as the responsible one; the saved one. You will take on our story and start to wear it like a second skin. A few years will pass and you will step into a new life. You will make good use of every moment; squeeze out every drop. You'll leave the home and become an actress on television. You'll be beautiful, with your long hair and long white hands. You'll have a dog and a cat and two children and a husband. You'll buy a new house and do gardening and cooking. Your children will be popular at school. You'll keep photos of them in frames arranged about the room, and when people ask you questions, you'll glance at the pictures with a loving look in your eye.

You'll never wake up in the morning and think that you are of no use to anyone. That whether you stay in bed or get up, it won't matter.

Sometimes you'll remember your friend. Nicola, who had silly ideas. You'll know there was nothing you could have done.

You see. It will be different for you, Jules. You'll have a wonderful life. And you will be so very, very happy.

Tweet Tweet
Anne Olerenshaw

On the fourth day the rangers found the abandoned vehicle on an old dirt track which had long since lost its way in this outback landscape. The driver's door gaped open, exposing the interior to the same thick red dust that caked wheels and paintwork. The radiator cap was on the bonnet. The helicopter moved on as the officers scanned the arid scene that stretched for miles in all directions. They were used to this harsh terrain, and familiar with the urges that led a few benighted souls into it, though it held no appeal for them. They were glad to have the means to return to base as they pressed on in search of their quarry, knowing he was out there, somewhere. But they could only guess what condition he might be in, if alive or dead.

'... must have dozed off for a while. Still with me, little bird, on your bare twig? Thanks for the company – you're all I've got left. How long has it been? Days, I think; time to reflect – try to come to terms with what I did. The anger's gone now, if it was anger – more like a frenzy that seized me – I behaved like a man possessed. But then they drove me to it. They deserved it, didn't they? So why am I still in hell? I was out of my mind at the time – that's one thing, but I can't deny I'd planned it – very carefully. What does that say about me? Once, I believed I was a civilised human being trying to lead a normal life. Now I'm an outcast, a guilty thing, rotting away in this god-forsaken place, waiting for the end, whatever that might be – dehydration, possibly, or capture by the law. Who knows? At least I've got you, little bird; size isn't everything.

'I should have given myself up like a man, but then I couldn't be sure if I was man or beast. All I remember are the primitive terrors that gripped me after that demented act. Why am I telling you all this when I know you can't understand a word of it? Maybe that's why. Anyway, I fled – out of the room where they'd been wallowing in their lust, where they'd felt safe, believing I'd never find them; racing from that house and away from their screams as fast as a madman could go. I can still hear those screams. What do you think of that, bird? A coward as well as a fiend? That's right, ruffle your feathers – get some air into those wings.

'Not much fresh air in this searing heat, but what did I expect?

At least nothing much can hurt me now, unless you count life imprisonment – a relief, if anything. Or dying of thirst under this leafless tree, with you looking on at me with those ancient beady eyes; but that shouldn't take too long. Otherwise, I'm impervious – that's a good word. If only I could have been impervious before. But I was desperate. Jealous suspicions welled up in me. I lost control. A wiser man might have walked away or thrown her out; instead, I blew a fuse. It's too late for regrets. I was besotted with her, and no mistake.

'How did she expect to deceive me for so long? I knew what she was up to. Well, I was almost sure I knew, but she went on denying it; claimed I was imagining things, paranoid even. Then she'd be very sweet and loving, until I felt like an ungrateful, love-crazed fool. You, my feathered friend, will never understand, however much you listen and stare.

'So I let it go for a while, tried to play it cool, though all hell was breaking loose underneath. She must have felt secure in my self-delusion because what I didn't know, you see, was who – who to suspect she was with, while I was earning the means to keep her looking sleek and stylish. She was clever at concealing her secret lover.

'I found out, though. Oh yes. I went out of my way to find out who it was. I knew there had to be someone else; it was only a question of time before I would catch them in the act. Since then, slumped here for days, I've had time to give it more thought

'What if I goaded her into it? What if my endless questions, my "whining", as she called it, my efforts to keep her out of the sight of other men, brought about what I dreaded most? I can't think any more. I need water. How do you manage to survive, bird? You brought me here, remember? I followed you into this wasteland, expecting you would lead me to water, somehow. What a stupid notion! There's nothing but a dried-up creek. Here we are, then, neither of us going anywhere beyond this tree.

'How could I blame her? She was so lovely. It was all those hungry stares that followed her everywhere, men always ogling her, waiting for the chance to steal her from me. What woman wouldn't be flattered by such attentions? Yet those eyes, so bright and sincere, seemed to be for me alone. When did that change? In my mind, I still see the eyes more clearly than all her other charms: the curves, the fine skin, the wonderful smile. All gone. You've become my only reality – you, ugly black bird with your staring yellow eyes. Not much charm there, friend.

'My only desire, now, is to die in peace, and I probably could if it weren't for the plagues of flies and ants and that blazing ball of nuclear

16

fusion up there. Still, it's just bearable, even with a mouth like a bowl of sawdust and lips like a couple of barbecued sausages. I could laugh at that thought but my vocal chords are rusting up – hardly a whisper left. My body is one silent demand for water, but I must get everything out before the end comes.

'It's my own fault, of course. I'd been warned of the dangers often enough. "Don't go alone into the bush, but if you do, tell someone where you'll be and when you'll be back. If you break down, stay on the road with the vehicle. Drink the radiator water if you must, but the essential thing is to stay put and wait for help." What's so difficult about that? It's a hard lesson to learn, but here, the penalty for disobedience is death within three or four flesh-roasting days – the wages of sin. Very fitting.

'Soon enough, though, if the police don't find me, I'll be unconscious and it won't matter. The muscles are already stiffening, so I can hardly move. I feel I'm shrinking into the earth, and while I shrink you get bigger – more like a crow than a sparrow. Well, my eyes aren't what they were a few days ago.

'Oh yes, the eyes. Was she really sweet and sincere, my soul-mate, my sensual lover, the girl of my dreams? Was she goddess or gold-digging nympho? Was it before or after we moved to this wilderness that she met and mated with that gigolo? As I remember it, she was very happy to come out here with me, encouraged me, even; said my career would be enhanced if I brought my "executive expertise" to bear on this new project, make an early foray into an untapped market. Did she say that or did I? Sounds a bit pompous, now. Either way, there'd be more in it for her when I got the pay-off. We celebrated, we drank to the future, I bought a pair of eternity rings, seriously expensive, but affordable for a top man in a petroleum company, and definitely going places. Stop croaking, you hideous, feather-brained creature. Whatever made me think you were my friend?

'The drink gets to you out here – the alcoholic kind, of course. I'm surprised they find enough water to dilute it with. Not that I found much need to dilute it after a while, after my suspicions started to grow. I blame it for our big row, along with my belief that she was cheating on me while I was busy swelling the bank account. I shouted, she shouted, I shouted again and it went on until I hit her. My ring, the twin to hers, tore a shred of skin from her cheek. It bled and she clutched at it and cried, while I felt mortified and afraid.

'It wasn't much of an injury but it changed everything – that sudden, shocking awareness that she was flesh and blood. How stupid could I be? She dragged her own ring from her finger and flung it down.... now I'm ranting; wasting energy – but it was a terrible moment. You still listening to me, bird? The sun has become a pulsating, caustic yellow, like your evil, hooded eyes. For God's sake, go away!

'Cracks in the earth are getting wider. Or is it my blurred vision? Open up and let me in; it has to be cooler down there, dust-dry but cool and safe, where flies can't drain the last trace of sweat from my skin... Oh, it's hopeless. I must try to think – keep the brain working.

'As chemist-cum-boardroom whizz-kid, I know all about fluids. Water: oxygen and hydrogen – necessary to all known life forms – turned into steam by heat and to ice by cold (not much chance of that around here). Whisky: usually malted barley distilled into spirituous liquor – my favourite tipple (single malt, of course). Blood: a viscous fluid composed of plasma with red and white cells to carry oxygen around the body. Oleum: a concentrated form of sulphuric acid, sometimes called vitriol, especially as a metaphor for malice – there's more malice in your cruel eyes, bird, than I've seen in a long time.

'You can sway there flapping those great wings, mocking and accusing me. I know what you're thinking. Yes, it was a foul act. I crept up on them while they were naked and vulnerable. I'd guessed what I would find but I should have stayed calm. I could have shown contempt, taunted them, then walked away and cut her out of my life. Instead, I was maddened by the sight of them locked in each other's arms. True, I'd planned what I might do – even prepared the means – I confess it, Your Honour – but it hadn't seemed real. Once in their little love-nest, seeing them together, I reacted almost on impulse. It took me just a second to position myself, and a second more for them to jerk round in terror. Then I did it, taking only a second to toss the vitriol into their faces, and another two to listen to the flesh sizzling on contact – and even to wince as the corrosive acid sucked the moisture from her delicate skin.

'I can hardly bear to think of it now. There's no point trying to imagine the shrivelled flesh, the blinded eyes, the pain. As for him, I can't bring myself to care. I've tried to feel some remorse but my mind keeps playing tricks on me and I'm no longer sure of the difference between fact and fantasy.

'I just wait here, then, while the shadows close over me. The light is reduced to chinks of sparkle between dark feathers. The brooding monster waits, too, dilating eyes, contracting talons, whetting the long beak. My strength is almost gone. Oh, God, help me....!'

The tree was one of the few natural features able to survive years of drought in the parched soil, so even from a distance it was easy to spot, as was the possible shape of a human body beneath it. They knew it had to be him. After landing, they approached the inert form and saw how the thin cotton shirt and jeans were stained and ragged around the sun-blistered limbs. And then they saw his face – what had been a face. Curiously, the hair-line was still intact, delineating the dust-matted scalp, but from forehead to chin, from ear to ear, what was left of the soft tissue was in tatters, as though the job of stripping it had been botched. But the orifices were clear – the nose area was a clown's black triangle, the eyes empty sockets and the lower jaw flopped open as if caught in the act of grinning at a huge joke. Ants and flies crawled in and out of these holes, about their business of collecting bits of brain from the skull. As the two officers recoiled, gagging, a few small black feathers fluttered briefly around the body.

Frank Solomon
Jack Rosenthal

In sleepless post-midnight exhaustion the relentless *tap-tap-tap* became a slow torture. Intermittently a comforting stillness would deliver the hope that old Frank next door had at last fallen asleep in his chair. Or, with his two sticks, had levered himself across the kitchen to his bed. Or maybe died. Sometimes, masochistically, I timed the intervals, silently counting: at twenty the hope would begin to strengthen (twenty-four, twenty-five) – silence – (twenty-six: thank God he's stopped, twenty-seven) then (O God!) *tap-tap-tap*, signalling that Frank had positioned the next apple log on his hearth and little by little was rendering it to kindling under the unceasing strokes of an antique billhook. Despairing of sleep I would pull down the pillow over my head with a sideways squint at a bedside clock that crawled through the dead hours toward dawn.

Not that Frank was trying to be unneighbourly: it was simply that his internal clock was beholden neither to any external one nor to the natural rhythm of sunrise and sunset. Throughout the day sleep stalked his brittle frame where it sat in a hardback chair by a blacked kitchen range, periodically overwhelming it, usurping any plan he might have had to actually go to bed. And when, with a shiver and shake, Frank re-awoke, at whatever hour, he would bend forward over the hearth to continue his eternal task of splitting the apple logs the foreman brought down from the grubbed orchards of the farm. Obsessively splitting them into ever thinner sticks to be fed into the firebox of the stove. Keeping his small withered body warm. *Tap-tap-tap*. Three in the afternoon or three in the morning, summer or winter, it was all the same to Frank.

His few needs were arranged around him within arms' reach. A loaf of sliced white bread, seedless jam, margarine, a pack of Bakewell tarts and another of processed ham lay on the small table beside his chair and were replenished by his carer, Mrs Bloomfield, on Mondays, Wednesdays and Fridays when she came in to do the necessary. On his other side a .410 shotgun was propped in the corner by the range, an old fold-in-half poacher's model with skeleton stock and a single barrel speckled with rust. Next to it stood a paper sack of wheat into which Frank would sporadically delve a wooden scoop, flicking the corn past the open back door to his few ageing hens which had no hesitation in crossing the threshold to follow the trail of grain to his slippered feet. Beneath the table a chamber pot served for those occasions when Frank's dicky legs were not up to the struggle to reach the privy outside. The fowls occasionally eyed the contents curiously but had the sense not to explore further.

The gun was for the rats that thrived secretively but with great fecundity in the wilderness of once-garden that crowded up against Frank's back door, a brambly jungle pierced only by the short, narrow tunnel of trodden-earth path leading to the brick outhouse. The rats' success was partly due to the largesse of corn and food scraps which they boldly appropriated from under the beaks of the chickens. This brazen theft annoyed Frank who, on spotting a rodent, would let fly with the .410 from where he sat by the stove. Unfortunately the coordination of the old poacher's rheumy eyes and unsteady hands were not as once they had been with the usual result that, as the rat scuttled off into the undergrowth unhurt, the shot would rake through the unsuspecting chickens, one or more of which would be left twitching on the path mortally wounded. Cursing, Frank would struggle to the fatality and hurl it away into the bushes. As the chickens decreased so the rats increased, a sort of win-win situation from their point of view.

But it was when it became necessary to talk to Frank for some reason or other that the path to his door became seriously dangerous. On these occasions I would squeeze through a gap in the bushes behind the outhouse before flattening myself against its rear wall and, with head turned sideways, extend a waving hand into the space above the path while shouting:

'Frank, it's me! Don't shoot!' like some gunslinger in a bad Western. Stepping out onto the path was always an anxious moment.

Although Frank callously discarded the martyred hens as too old and tough to bother with, his night-time roamings of earlier years had left him with a great fondness for roast pheasant. Late in the year these would be attracted to their favoured roosting sites in the tangled thorn bushes behind Frank's half of the cottage, the cocks always foolishly announcing their presence by crowing as they fluttered up in the dusk. This usually proved too much for Frank, who would hobble down the path on only one stick, his other arm crooked around the .410. Propping himself against the trunk of a dead apple tree or the outhouse wall he would raise the gun toward the silhouetted bird, quietly cock the hammer and pull the trigger. Sometimes the pheasant would fall dead through the branches, sometimes Frank would fall unbalanced into the undergrowth. As the season wore on it became touch and go as to who was at greatest risk of death, man or bird, until eventually the procedure became that Frank would summon me with a double knock on the wall. In his kitchen he would thrust the loaded gun at me with something like: 'There's a cock-bird gone up at the far end of the hedge, boy. Just go and get it for me.'

By January there were never many left.

Frank plucked these pheasants sitting in his chair by the range. The upward draught of heat would waft the downy under-feathers into a gentle grey snowstorm that settled over the room, sizzling on the hotplate, sticking to the margarine tub and the plates in the sink and coating the bed with a thin, freelance eiderdown. Most of the feathers proper Frank shoved into the firebox of the range, producing a crematorium-like smell; the guts were thrown out through the door to be recycled by the chickens and rats, and the carcase itself went into the oven. A neat and very localised energy cycle.

One November day in 1979 I ran the gauntlet of the path to let Frank know that early in the new year I would be moving to another tied cottage a few miles away in Heveningham. He averted his eyes: 'Huh! Yew on't like it.'

'Why not, what's the matter with Heveningham?' I retorted, defensively. 'You spent your whole working life in Peasenhall, just down the road from there!'

'They're a bloody rum lot. You'll see,' said Frank with assumed authority, signalling the end of the exchange.

A day or two later Mrs Bloomfield was getting ready to leave on her shiny new moped as I arrived back at the cottage for lunch on my old push-bike.

'I hear you're leaving us,' she said inquisitively.

''Fraid so,' I replied. 'I've sorted out a better arrangement on a farm in Heveningham. Mind you, Frank seems to think it'll be worse.'

'Yes, well, that will be because of poor old Florrie,' said Mrs B. 'She married a pigman in Heveningham who turned out to be a right bad sort, knocked her about so they said. Then he ran off with the neighbour's wife in the middle of the night. Old man Wright had to feed the pigs himself for a week or two until he found a new man, then chucked Florrie out of the house without so much as a by your leave. She had to live in a one-up, one-down with Frank and his wife for years before she got a council flat in Ipswich. Far as Frank's concerned they're all tarred with the same brush.'

Florence was Frank's only child, a thin, chestless woman in her late sixties who had neither had children with the errant pigman nor remarried after his sudden leaving. On her rare visits to her father she usually wore a tired grey flannel skirt below a drooping button-front cardigan, the pockets stuffed with tissues. She bore the look of a woman for whom life had passed slowly with scant pleasure. As she didn't drive her visits were dependent on the good nature of a female acquaintance from the Methodists who brought her out from Ipswich. In any event there was little attraction, for when she did arrive the squalor of Frank's cottage upset her tidy mind, eventually provoking her to inquire at the council offices as to whether he might be moved into a home. We exchanged telephone numbers against the event of any urgent need to contact one another in relation to Frank.

No doubt as a result of Florrie's inquiries, one morning in early December a small red car was parked on the road outside Frank's half of the cottage while its driver, a pert young woman with short black hair and an air of efficiency, cast her eyes around his kitchen as she ticked boxes on a form headed *Assessment for Residential Care: Critical Score Sheet*. Questions were grouped under headings such as *Cooking Facilities*, *Personal Hygiene Arrangements* and *Mobility*. At its end a large space had been allocated for *Officer Comments* and here at the end of a lengthy paragraph of neat handwriting the young woman had noted: *Some sort of gun is present and appears unsecured*. From this sentence an arrow guided the reader's eye to the margin where she had added in smaller writing: *Refer to relevant authority*.

This she must have done, for one day the following week a police car was parked where the council officer's had been, its garish checkering a little unnerving as my mind raced over possible failures in licences, tyres, road tax, dogs, guns. As soon as I had entered my half of the cottage Frank's double knock summoned me to his kitchen where a large policeman in a black vest decorated with a two-way radio and silver numbers explained that by rights, as Mr Solomon had no shotgun certificate, he should confiscate the shotgun then and there. That was the law. But Mr Solomon had proposed that perhaps I could take charge of the weapon forthwith and take it into Richardsons' gunsmiths in Halesworth to see if I could at least obtain a few pounds to compensate Mr Solomon for its loss. In his chair Frank was jiggling one of his sticks up and down between his knees, a sure sign of agitation, for the policeman had tactlessly pointed out that the gun might as well go as it certainly wouldn't be allowed in the nursing home. Talk of any imminent move to a nursing home was news to Frank. Though he did remember Mrs B. had said something about her rota possibly being rearranged. Bureaucracy was closing in on Frank; a sense of inevitability began to pervade his thoughts.

Two days later, pruning up in the orchards, it did not seem particularly surprising to hear a siren approaching the village and then stop. At the cottage the police car was back. But beside it an ambulance with open rear doors blocked the road, its lights still silently flashing. In the back of it I could see Mrs B. sitting on a bench seat: a blanket was over her shoulders, her hands to her face. A paramedic was kneeling in front of her proffering a mug of tea. The same policeman was sitting in the passenger seat of his car, his legs out through the open door, talking into his radio. Looking up at me he broke off: 'Don't go in there. There's been an incident: the old boy's shot himself. Forensic's on the way from Martlesham.'

Nausea welled. He turned back to the radio: 'Yeah, blood everywhere, right mess.'

On the concrete pathway to the front gate wet boot-prints like dark woodcuts were drying to black, gruesomely confirming his report.

There were a lot of phone calls, a lot of questions over the next few days; some sort of police inquiry looked likely. Mrs B. was positive it was an accident, surprised it hadn't happened long ago: the gun was always loaded, the hammer loose, Frank doddery. And the shot had been to the neck, not in the mouth or head. But did it matter? The gun should not have been there: mistakes had been made: answers were needed. Then on Christmas Eve I answered the phone to a cheerful woman's voice: 'Oh, I am sorry to bother you on Christmas Eve, but we've got this number in connection with a Mr Solomon. We can't seem to contact his daughter, but we were expecting Frank here in time for Christmas. We're holding a room for him but we've heard absolutely nothing.'

'Sorry, but who are you?' I asked.

'This is the Meadow View Nursing Home in Heveningham.'

Blood Type
Rosemary Smith

I was once told that warm milk, straight from the cow, is as ambrosia compared to the UHT stuff you get in cartons these days. My mouth feels furry. I probe my cheeks with my tongue and press it against the sharp edges of my teeth. The blood has gone but I can still recall the taste, rich and heavy with metallic undertones. I was lucky not to have lost a tooth. The bugger gave me a bloody nose too; the remains cracked and hardened on my skin. I struggle up stiffly out of my nest, run some water and wash my face. My next thought the realisation, accompanied by a great wave of relief, that I'm happy to be a UHT-type man. I confess that I live off ready meals.

It all began several months ago. Being retired I volunteer evenings in the library, having had a lifelong love of books and now equally fascinated by what can be discovered on the Internet.

I was re-shelving late one Friday when I felt a gentle tug at my elbow. Startled, I looked down to see a young girl; huge vulnerable brown eyes and straight mouth. A wise imp, neatly dressed in private school tie, white socks and modest, long, blond ponytail.

'Excuse me,' she said hesitantly.

People usually avoid me. I was savaged by a dog as a child and in those days the only treatment was the herbs and poultices of the village midwife. I lost my eye and to offset the patch that covers the scars I have developed a theatrical style of dressing – cravats, lilac jackets, large brimmed hats, that sort of thing. For special occasions I have a black cape and a silver-topped cane. I'm immune now to hostile stares and furtive glances; I know what people are thinking. I don't particularly mind; I am by nature a solitary creature and I always know where to find company if I feel the need. I smiled. The child didn't seem to be put off.

'I hope you don't mind; can you tell me what "iota" means?'

She proffered her book, *To Kill a Mockingbird*.

'I know it's nearly closing time and the other librarian has cleared my dictionary away,' she gabbled on, a nervous edge in her voice, 'and if I get it out again she'll just think I'm being a nuisance.'

'It means a tiny bit,' I said.

'Thank you.' She returned to her seat.

I noticed that she waited until the very last minute before pulling on her coat and scarf, shouldering her school bag and walking slowly to the front door. I was standing waiting to say goodnight to Mrs Beauchamp, who was turning out the last of the lights.

'Is someone collecting you?' I asked the girl.

'No, I'm walking,' she said and pushed open the glass door. I followed her out. The alleyways beside the shops were already filling with evil-drinking spirits.

'Where do you live?' I asked.

'South Hill Road.'

'It's on my way,' I lied; 'I'll walk you home.'

'That's OK,' she replied. 'I'll be fine.'

'But it's dark and late, you shouldn't be out on your own.'

'It's very kind of you but I'll get in trouble for talking to strangers.'

'I insist. I would feel ashamed if anything happened to you and I hadn't done my duty,' I said and gave a little bow.

She giggled, her breath curling in plumes.

'Look, I've been checked, have to work here, and I'll tell Mrs Beauchamp, so you know I can be trusted. OK?'

'OK,' she replied.

Mrs Beauchamp nodded curtly and locked the library door behind us.

'What's your name?' I asked as we set off.

'Milly,' she replied.

'Nice to meet you Milly. You can call me Mr Pickles,' I said.

'Mr Pickles? That sounds like a made-up name.'

'It is.'

'Well what's your real name?'

'It's foreign and terribly hard to pronounce.'

She laughed again. It was beautiful, like moonlight helter-skelter through a wind chime.

We chattered quite easily, Milly happy to talk about the books she was reading and I happy to make further recommendations, surprised and impressed by the number of times she came back to me with: 'I've read that already.'

She stopped at the fish and chip shop and came out with a steaming portion.

'Want one?' she asked sucking cold air over the hot chip in her mouth.

'No thanks.'

'You don't like chips!'

'No.'

'No wonder you're so pale and skinny.'

We walked on, the shops giving way to suburban streets.

'How old are you Milly?'

'Eleven. How old are you?'

'How old do you think I am?'

She peered at my face. It felt a little uncomfortable, having her study it so closely.

'Oh dear,' I said after seconds of silence, 'that old?'

'I'd say forty-seven.'

'Ah, you're just trying to flatter me.'

'How old are you then?'

'Five hundred and seventy-two next birthday.'

She giggled deliciously.

'Who's your best friend?' I asked.

'Marmite, my cat,' she replied without hesitation. 'Who's yours?'

'Mrs Beauchamp.'

'No she isn't.'

I cocked my head.

'It's not fair if I tell you and you don't tell me.'

'Alright,' I said. 'His name was Ettore, but he died a long time ago. Right now you're my best friend.'

As we approached her house her chattering slowed and then stopped and she walked leadenly. The house was detached, three stories, a large wooden front door with iron braces, an Audi and a Range Rover on the gravel drive. What kind of well-to-do parents would treat their own precious flesh and blood so casually? Allowing her to walk home alone at night through city streets where muggings were as common as eye teeth.

She turned to me at the start of the drive.

'Thank you,' she said.

'You're welcome,' I replied and, realising that this was a dismissal, tipped my hat and turned. I walked away a few paces and then paused to watch her safely in.

She was greeted by her mother, a large-hipped blonde lady in slippers who smiled appeasement and who, instead of a cardigan, wore a wrap of anxiety around her hunched shoulders. The door shut quickly; Milly didn't look back.

I went hopefully to the library every night the following week, and muffled my disappointment at Milly's absence by searching for books that I thought she would like.

To my delight she reappeared on Friday and even seemed pleased to see me.

The walk home on a Friday evening quickly became the highlight of my week. I adored Milly's beguiling laughter and childish frankness and I rapidly became very fond of her. But I could sense there was something amiss. She was like a blanket of snow in a churchyard; pretty, soft and fresh but at the same time covering a great sadness. I asked her about friends and family but she would not be drawn. Books were the only thing she opened up with. I tried the trick she'd used on me – 'it's not fair if I tell you…', but she simply replied: 'Life's not fair.' Which, in her sweet silver voice, struck me as sadly grown up and cynical. She always said goodbye at the driveway, never invited me to meet her Mum and Dad. That was OK. I hate hovering politely on doorsteps not knowing what to say.

There came one night after several weeks when Milly seemed more reluctant than usual to go home. As we started our walk she put on a limp so obviously fake that I could barely conceal my smile.

'What's the matter Milly? Have you hurt your leg?'

'Someone bashed it at school with a hockey stick.'

When we passed the fish and chip shop she was several paces behind me. I turned to see her gazing in through the window.

'I'm going in to get some chips,' she said.

'OK,' I replied. I stood outside and waited and after a few minutes, when she did not return, I realised she had sat down inside to eat them. I went in and sat opposite her, squinting in the sudden brightness. She ate slowly, blowing the heat out of each chip and taking tiny mouthfuls.

'Won't your mum be worried that you're home so late?' I asked her.

'She's changed her hours.'

'But it's nearly nine o'clock; isn't your dad at home?'

She looked at me blankly and sniffed.

'What time does your mum get home?'

'Ten thirty.'

'And your dad?'

'We don't get on.'

'Is that why you don't want to go home?'

She stared at the table.

'But you can't sit in the fish and chip shop 'til then.'

'I can if I like,' she replied, suddenly hostile.

'Can't your mum give you a key so you can let yourself in?'

'I've got a key. Anyway, why are you so interested all of a

sudden?'

'I'm sorry,' I said. 'It's none of my business. Would you still like me to walk you home?'

'I don't care, you can do what you like.'

I was puzzled and upset by this sudden change. Over the weeks I felt that we had become friends. This was a new sensation and it excited me. At my age there is very little new to experience in life; now I was left feeling stupid and embarrassed, assuming that such a young girl would want to be friends with an old man. Our shared love of literature an illusion, two people staring in the same mirror, but each only able to see one reflection – Milly's.

We finally got to her house, awkwardly, ten o'clock by the pole star. After we said good night I hid out of sight. I watched her shivering amongst the hawthorn in the front garden until the headlights of the Range Rover rumbled along the road and she dashed into the house ahead of her mother.

The next week there was a similar charade but when we arrived home both cars were on the drive. Milly seemed surprised. I watched her go cautiously to the front door but it wasn't her mother that opened it. A tall man in shirt and tie grabbed her by the shoulder and yanked her indoors. Milly squealed. The large door slammed.

Now I may be old but I have an acute sense of hearing. I could still hear the screaming from behind the door. I floated stealthily across the gravel drive. The man's voice rattled the kitchen window at the side of the house.

Peering through from the shadows I could see him holding a sheaf of soggy papers in one hand and in the other a wriggling black cat, dangling by the scruff just above the hot plate of the Aga. Milly was hysterical, crying and begging. The man blazed at her, his face red fury, then dropped the cat. The howl was bloodcurdling. Milly fell to her knees, the man grabbed her pony tail and dragged her from the room. In the bedroom above the screaming stopped.

Light as a bat and silent as mist, I hung outside the window.

Milly was sobbing quietly on the bed, curled up like a fetus. Her father ranted his disgust.

'And I'll have to replace the printer. You can spend the whole weekend in this bedroom writing out my lecture. I need fifty copies. That cat has peed its last. I'm sick to death of the stinking filthy thing. It's going down the vet's first thing and it won't be coming home.'

The thought of this vile man inflicting such unjust punishment on my innocent young friend reignited a primeval outrage I had forgotten existed. I acted impulsively, instinctively and appeared in the room before him. My first concern was that Milly must not see this. My hand on her head, a brief incantation and she was instantly asleep.

The man's face turned from masochistic rage to startled horror. I smiled, only partly because of the comic nature of so rapid a change of expression. Clearly petrified of me, he could have had no idea how nervous I was feeling; like waiting to do a practical exam you're several hundred years too late for. I hadn't done this since the reckless days of my youth; not for five hundred and fifty years.

The man fled down the wide carpeted stairway. I followed him, trying to resist panic myself, my hand calmly sliding on the banister.

He emerged from an office room brandishing a small gun as I stepped off the bottom stair. The gun jiggled uselessly in his hand. He fired twice. I grabbed his neck in my left hand; that's when he head butted me. I felt that. Not pain, which came later, just the impact. And then I sank my teeth into his neck. The warm blood flowed freely, too fast. I couldn't swallow it all; it ran off my chin and soaked his shirt.

When he was dead I picked up the gun and shot him where the bite mark was, dialled 999 and left. Milly would sleep for hours; the police would be baffled.

My face feels smooth now, all the blood has gone. The sensation of outrage from the previous night has disappeared, the moment of madness passed. In that way I feel normal again. Milly is free of her hideous father. I'm sure he must have had good life cover, I reason, to smother an annoying twinge of guilt. My main worry is that in all the fuss that is bound to follow no one will think to take Marmite to the vet to see to her burnt paws. Maybe I could pass by coincidentally and volunteer. I'm in such a good mood I might even wear my cape. I love the swish of the red satin lining. I open the fridge, more out of habit than because I am hungry. I still feel bloated, hungover almost. The blood bags are all lined up neatly. I get them from the hospital; once they've passed their use-by date, still perfectly edible. They're all treated, you see, just like UHT.

The Bonds That Bind
Sultan Walpole

Alice: As I look down at my swollen stomach, I resist the instinctive urge I have to smooth the bulge that I suspect is caused by a hand or a foot. I try not to pay too much attention to my stomach when I am with Claire, who doesn't understand or approve of my detachment. I see the way she wrings her hands, fiddles with her hair, jams her hands into her pockets – anything to resist the compulsion she has to touch my belly. There are times when she can't help it, her hands trembling as they smooth over my 'bump', as she calls it. She opens her mouth to speak, but words fail her. I stand there, an intruder in her most intimate moment.

'Bump.' What an insignificant word for the stretching and tearing of skin. My body has become a route map to an unfamiliar place; the torn flesh, the swollen contours, the once familiar now obscured from view.

'You should try it,' I feel like telling her, 'you should try the sleepless nights and the mad hormones. You wouldn't look so starry-eyed then.' But I don't say that, of course. What I do say is, 'Yes, they are moving about a fair bit today...' 'No, I haven't forgotten to take my vitamin supplements...' 'Yes, they did say you could come to the next scan.'

Despite herself, she cannot hide the look of concern that flashes across her face as she offers me a cup of decaf tea and I ask for a bottle of beer. She stammers that she has no alcohol-free beer and I give her a look, one that says, 'Why would I want alcohol-free beer?' She can't deny me, so off she trots to the immaculate kitchen in her period house and returns with a trendy Habitat glass frosted with cold beer.

'It would have been fine in the bottle,' I tell her, inexplicably annoyed at this small gesture of what is, after all, simple hospitality. I won't drink all of it, though. Just a sip. I just like to see the look on her face when I ask for it. I'll tip the rest of it into the plant pot by the side of the sofa when she's not looking.

I'm not cruel by nature, but I find that circumstances have put me in a position where, unusually, I have the upper hand over Claire. I have tried not to abuse my power, but she has made it hard for me not to – I've never known her to be so compliant. But then the stakes have never been so high.

When Claire first told me she had had four miscarriages, caused by a rare condition that meant she could not carry her babies in her womb, I'm ashamed to say that my first thoughts were, 'Of course it would be *rare*. Claire Jennings wouldn't be seen dead with a *common* condition.' The thought was shocking, even to me.

Claire was always the radiant one. She had inherited our mother's good looks; her golden hair and beauty drew people to her. Growing up had been effortless for her. She had not been troubled by acne, braces or a flat chest. She had left us, Mum, Dad and I, far behind as she blazed a trail though university and then, later, the world of banking. I had watched from the sidelines, graced occasionally with the rays of her presence as I helped Mum and Dad with the business in the early years, and then nursed them in the later years. I hadn't seen her since our mother's funeral two years earlier. Since then, contact between us had been via an infrequent exchange of emails, even though she only lived twenty miles away. So I had been shocked to see her usually glowing features pale and drawn with stress and anxiety, clearly more dependent on her brash husband Gerry than she ever had been before. I felt only pity for her and embarrassment at my own callousness. She had never needed me so much.

And so it had happened in a smart Harley Street clinic, followed by a stay in an expensive hotel in London. Initially, there was little to say once we had got past the euphoria of the positive pregnancy test result. They promised me anything and everything and even offered to fund the holiday of a lifetime for me. They were supportive and kind, until Claire decided she needed to be more in control of the situation. That was when the trouble started.

The more she interfered and told me what I should be doing, the more I resisted, until we became again the teenagers we once were, although this time we did not have Mum and Dad to 'knock our heads together', as Dad used to say. The more she wanted me to do the 'right' things during the pregnancy, the less likely I was to do them in her presence. I read the books and magazines alone, at home, and I found myself increasingly less interested in the tidy and orderly life I had settled on, and more interested in the rhythms of my body, changing internally and externally. The bonds of flesh connecting me to the babies so tenuous, so transitional.

Now, Claire fusses around me, offering me another cushion for my aching back, a footstool for my swollen feet. I complain about the horrendous smell coming from the plug- in air freshener near the sofa and she hurriedly switches it off, wafting the air to get the smell away from me. I try to hide a small smile of satisfaction. I should enjoy the attention, I suppose, but I never asked for it and I certainly didn't expect that Claire would give it so willingly.

As I sink back into her designer sofa, I close my eyes, to try and shut out the sight of her picking up one of the many pregnancy books and magazines arranged neatly on her coffee table. It's only a matter of time before she starts reading out an article that she thinks will be of benefit to me. I know it's absurd to think this and maybe the pregnancy has turned my mind to mush, but I'm sure that the babies are listening to her, absorbing her voice. She pauses reading halfway through the article and looks up to see if I'm listening, if I'm taking it all in and I pretend to have fallen asleep.

Claire: She makes me so angry. How can she be so blasé about this pregnancy? About the two lives she is carrying and nurturing inside her body? I'm doing everything I can for her, and more, but she's as difficult as ever. She has always been like this with me, sullen and uncooperative. A martyr.

Even now, when she has something that I can only dream about, a healthy pregnancy and two lives growing inside her, she pretends to be uninterested. It was like this when we were growing up, Mum and her with their easy banter and cosy chats over coffee. Insignificant bits of information that she would keep from me to show her superiority over me. Now this. Her pretend detachment is driving me insane and she knows it. I could hit her. I came close to it one night, when early in the pregnancy I had been ringing her all night and she had not picked up her phone. I was worried out of my mind that something bad had happened. Finally, Gerry and I had driven round to her flat. We had found her there, eating chocolate and watching a movie as the lights on the answer phone blinked the desperate messages I had left for her.

She had been nonchalant, amused even, at my distress and had told me to 'get a grip'. I have never been so angry. Fortunately, Gerry had stepped in, assuring Alice that our concern was only for her welfare and for that of the babies. After that, he had literally frogmarched me out of the flat. I had spent the journey home worried that Alice would change her mind; after all, it had not been too late at that time for a termination.

As I had arrived home, my phone had rung. It was Alice. 'Just thought you would like to know that I felt a bit of movement inside after you left. It was funny, like butterfly wings – just like the feeling you read to me from that book.' That was it. Alice's version of an apology.

Now, she's lying there with her half-empty glass of beer at her side, pretending to be asleep, ignoring me as I read to her about the importance of classical music to a developing baby. My gaze leads to her bump, where my babies are snug together, growing in a body that does not belong to their mother. My heart tightens in my chest as I notice some movement on her bump and I yearn to reach over and touch it; to wrap my arms around her stomach and to whisper to my babies, so they can hear my voice, so that they know me, their mother, when they are born.

Alice: I decide to leave as soon as I sense her desperation, her need to touch my stomach. 'To connect', as she puts it, and I suppose I can't blame her. Still, I'm doing enough just carrying the babies for her. She can hardly expect me to let her touch me as she pleases. We were never a touchy feely kind of family.

I get a massive headrush as I stand up too quickly and I am glad for Claire's support as she jumps to my side. My gratitude soon wears thin as her fussing begins to get on my nerves and I tell her that I'm going home.

'Really? Are you sure you're well enough?'

'Yes, I'm fine. Where did you put my coat?' I head out into the hall, my sights on the road now that I've made up my mind to leave.

'You could stay here tonight. You know you're always welcome to stay until the babies come.' She blushes, adding, 'And for a time after that, of course.'

'Thanks, but I'll go home. Where's my coat?' I repeat.

'Right here,' she says pulling it out of the hall closet. 'If you just give me a moment, I'll get my coat and walk you to your car.'

I tell her to stop making a fuss, and leave without giving her a chance to protest. It is the look of desolation that crosses her face as she kisses me goodbye and pats my stomach as I turn to leave that occupies my mind on the way home.

I want her to be happy, of course I do, or why else would I have agreed to do this?

By the time I let myself into my little flat, bought with my share of the money after Mum's death, my stomach feels tight and I am tired. As I go to the kitchen to get myself a glass of water, the babies move again, and now that I am alone, I am free to enjoy it – not too much, of course I could never allow that, but just enough so that I find I am dancing slowly up and down my narrow kitchen, singing a lullaby I have not heard since I was a child. I convince myself that the babies are enjoying this, so I go into the living room where there is more space and put on Classic FM. We dance together, I and my babies who are not really mine at all.

It is then that I feel water between my legs and I am embarrassed to find that I have peed myself. I sit on the floor and laugh. 'You'll never want to come and visit an aunt who smells of wee, will you?' I ask the babies, though I start to worry when the dribbles turn to a big rush of fluid. Too scared to look down, I put my hand between my legs, relieved to find no blood on my fingers when I bring them up to my face.

'My waters are breaking,' my rational self says: 'Call the hospital. Call Claire,' but I am fixed to the spot with the thought that the time for parting from the babies is near and I don't know how I will bear it.

As my stomach tightens with the first of many contractions, I feel the impatience of the babies in their sudden stillness. They have waited for this moment for an age and they are impatient to leave me and to go to their mother and that is okay, I tell myself. That is the natural order of things.

Claire: About an hour after Alice leaves to go home on the bus, a feeling of panic rises in my stomach. It's a feeling I haven't had since Alice and I were teenagers and I'd wake in the middle of the night with the inexplicable feeling that something was wrong; I'd go into Alice's room to find her writhing in pain from her period. I'd get her a hot water bottle and a paracetamol and sit with her for a while before going back to bed. As this memory comes back to me, I wonder how we became such strangers. With an unsteady hand, I dial her number, panic rising as she does not answer her phone. But this is not like the other times; this time she is not answering the phone because something is wrong and I feel this so strongly that before I know what I am doing I am in the car, screeching down the road. As I bang on her front door, I hear her whimper and I hold back a sob that rises to my throat.

'Alice. Alice, are you there?' I kneel to look through the letter box but I can see nothing as my eyes go black and I fear I am about to pass out when Alice opens the door. I find myself staring directly at her stomach as she looks down at me.

'Hold your horses,' she announces, her cheeks flushed, 'I'm only in labour!' Then, reaching out to help me up, she tells me, 'They're coming. They can't wait to meet you.' It is the loveliest thing she has

35

ever said.

'I knew it!' I gasp through my tears, and I am overwhelmed with a rush of emotion for my little sister. I would take her pain from her if I could, even if they were not my babies, and it dawns on me at last, why she has agreed to do this.

As we stand eye to eye, separated but united by the flesh and blood of the babies that are the strongest ties that we will ever share, I take her hand, pick up the hospital bag that I helped her to pack weeks ago and we walk to my car.

The Whale
Elspeth Latimer

The morning after the storm, word reached the Marine Stores. A dead whale had washed up on Carna Beach. The news spread from harbour to town, but it didn't find Tommy Nolan. His ears not being inclined for listening.

At five to nine he cycled past St Vincent's and kept on going. His mind on a promise no classroom could keep. Down the hill to the bridge, legs chasing the pedals. A whoop of delight through the door of O'Driscoll's, thinking to rouse his Father at the bar. Scrape of toe leather on tarmac as he neared the junction. The river past its spate, Mad Feeney eyeing up the spoil on the banks for a matching boot.

Tommy jerked his head for a final look at the straggle of houses. He'd finished the last of the milk. Had a worry what his Mother would put in her tea instead. He'd left her a slice of bread wrapped in a cloth. Taken the heel for his dinner. She'd never liked the crust, not even when Maeve was alive.

Fields between him and the sea. Fit for sheep and cattle and not much more, but green like no other green. Green, that when Mrs Clarey was scratching out long division on the board, he could just shut his eyes and see. And a wind, always a wind, tugging the grass this way and that in the shut of his eyes. A stiff one today, after the storm, filling his mouth as he panted up the rise. Shaping a windy tune with the stretch of his lips.

There was one bit of maths she'd learned him. Fractions. One in five. Mrs Clarey had told him if he kept his absence to once a week, then the school inspector would leave him alone. And her, more's to the point. Mother used to call her a lazy old so-and-so when it still seemed to matter.

He was on the high ground now, the ruined cottage still begging a roof. He'd made a castle of it, before another birthday came and the smell of cow shite killed his games. You're such a dreamer, Tommy boy, Father would say. A tingle on his scalp where Father used to ruffle his hair. That same hand better shaped now for raising a pint, Father's thirst a long one.

Up ahead he could see Tiller's. Slow on the brake, so as not to screech, Tommy stopped by the gate. Tiller's had two big windows in front, and two matching ones behind. You could look straight through to the water, framed and special. He ducked to his old height. Splitting the glass into halves of sky and blue. Sometimes he'd see the old man cross the horizon, from one window to the next. Once he'd seen him pull up a cabbage from a mess of weeds by the front door. Surprised to learn there was more to him than a tatty silhouette.

He liked Tiller's, but he feared it as well. Seeing right through to the other side. Nothing to hide. At home, Tommy went looking in the mirror. Staring into his eyes, straining to see out the other side. Proving to himself it wasn't his fault, because see, see, there's nothing to hide. But just like Tiller's, he knew a shadow was in there.

Tommy set off again, chin on the handlebars, stoking up a rush. On his left was the path belonged to the Strand where they raced the ponies. But Tommy had another beach in mind, beyond the Point. The Strand he saved for the wettest days, walking the length of the sand in search of a drenching. Thinking the rain an unnatural thing to be falling here, the sea had water enough. One thought at a time was all he had room for, and the nonsense ones were the best as they could last for hours.

The wind behind and both feet dangling, Tommy freewheeled it to the spring. Laid his bike by the ditch and climbed the hill. Water gushed from a crack of rock all frilled about with ferns. He splashed his face and neck, a sting in the breeze as he straightened up. The day had been softer that time he brought Maeve out here. His legs had ached when they got to the spring, what with cycling standing up and her perched on the saddle behind. Sliding about in her Sunday knickers and gripping his back with hands like pincers.

She'd loved that day, talking about it afterwards, on and on till Mother told her to hold her tongue. The happiest day of his life. He could say that without crossing his fingers.

Maeve was better company than boys his age. Tommy decided, long ago, that growing up was like sinking into that bog below Castle Mount. Once your legs were in you'd had it. A fence had been put around on account of the cattle but they still got in there. Word was, if you ever fell in, you had to pray to God there were the bones of a great big heifer to help you out.

Maeve kept the growing up at bay with her funny way of looking at things, all inside out and back to front. It was better her way round, and he used to hope she'd never change. Mother wouldn't let her go roaming, said she wasn't old enough. Besides, Maeve was her favourite. Tommy's too. Then that day had come when Mother was needed to do extra at the Grange, and Father away in Cork. Seeing as you're ten now, she'd said, giving him a look, like he was a boy from next door.

Mother had been shocked that he'd taken Maeve along the coast. But she hadn't told him not to. That went without saying, she'd said.

If Maeve hadn't had that day, her life would have been smaller still. Main Street, Infants' School and the paved backyard. Playing princess and ghosts with the washday sheets. As it was, she'd made a world in her head from that day on the beach.

We'll do it again, he'd said. Never mind about Mother. We'll go there again. Promise.

Mother was offered Mondays and glad to take it. Tommy could make himself useful, minding Maeve after school. But an hour wouldn't get them to Carna and back.

Tommy opened his eyes. He was flat on his stomach. Marestail and crowfoot scratching his face. A black beetle was picking its way over wet moss. With all his heart he wished he could be that beetle. Would take him a lifetime to get home from here. If wishing worked. Not even God's wishes came true.

He filled his bottle at the spring. Pushed the bike till he was ready to get back on. Worked his legs, soaking up the green as it sped past. He needed to store it up because he knew he'd be leaving. Soon as he could he'd be off. To England. They had a machine for everything. He wouldn't have to lift a finger.

Another mile and the sign was there, pointing down the boreen. Tommy left his bike, wasn't in the mood for a jolted arse. It was quiet in here, away from the wind. He followed the track as it carved its way to the sea. Clouds whipping overhead.

On the seventh day Father had pulled down the blinds. Six days of coast guard and search parties. All that time, Mother couldn't look at Tommy, her wet eyes sliding past. No son of hers. Did not speak to him once, except to say, 'You'll be better off indoors.'

No Maeve. They wouldn't even say her name. No news yet, was all he heard. Through open doors of rooms he wasn't welcome in.

Then on the seventh day Father pulled down the blinds in every room in the house. No funeral to be had.

'We have to show our respect,' he said. Mother wrenched his arms.

'It has to be done,' Father shouted, fighting her off. She turned away, sat down on a chair. Laid her head on the dowry table. Looking sideways across the mahogany. Not even a tear in her eyes. Just staring along the shine. The smell of polish followed Tommy up the stair. He clawed at the arms and legs that hadn't saved. But there'd been nothing to save.

They'd been standing on the pier, a swell on the grey sea. Maeve let go of his hand, to see what Brendan had in his lobster pots. Tommy followed close after. The tick of time that took her, from one second to the next, was the screech of a gull and him looking up at the sky. A heavy spray hit Tommy's face, he looked down and Maeve was gone. Dregs of sea washing off the pier. He'd run to the edge, screaming. Someone caught him as he was about to jump. Gripped him while his legs thrashed. People came running, shouting. Brendan leapt in with the life ring round his waist. Disappeared under the next wave, only his yellow slicker showing and the rope straining. Everyone yelling her name. Brendan gulping air and flailing his arms. They hauled him out after he struck the side, blood streaming down his face. Brendan had looked at Tommy and shaken his head.

Tommy used to hope she'd never change. He stumbled and opened his eyes, started running down the boreen. Careening from side to side, aiming for the brambles. Finally he hit the gate, with the first view of the beach. He climbed to the third rung, the wind slapping his hair. Tommy looked at the ragged coast and the gouge of Carna Bay. To north and south, a scatter of tiny islands tufted with green. He used to swim to them. Crown himself king.

The tide was on the ebb now, driving at the shore even on its way out. He swung his leg over the top of the gate.

His heart jumped. There on the beach below.

Maeve. Come home after seven months.

He yelled her name, straining to see.

Not Maeve as he knew her. But swollen with Mother's grief. Bloated with Father's whiskey tears, she'd grown so much.

Tommy shook his head. Climbed down from the gate. Maeve wouldn't look like that. She would be perfect.

At the end of the boreen, a gust sent him reeling. His bare ankles scoured with grit, he leaned on the wind, heading for the whale. Too big for a minke. It was a finback. Vast like a cow's grey tongue, humped on the butcher's slab, covered with a spittle of sand. He gave it a kick. It was solid as a house. He'd never seen this much flesh in one creature. Big like he was stood next to a hill. But not big enough to survive the storm. Not even a whale had managed that.

Tommy circled it, running his hands over blunt fins. Long flanks, like a submarine. Leather tail, flat on the sand. Sad mouth, clamped tight. Pucker of black where the eyes were shut. Tommy was glad of that. Didn't want to see its pain. He stroked the huge head. Pressed his cheek to skin that smelled of herring. Thought of the giant heart, inside the giant body.

Today he would do it.

In the lee of the whale, Tommy stripped off his clothes. He ran down the beach. Waded into the foamy sea, the water pulling at his calves. He pictured the whale alive, shoving aside the Atlantic with a bash of its tail. Tommy shaped his arms for a dive. A wave hit his stomach, splashed his face. Left a taste on his tongue.

Tommy rubbed his eyes. Went back up the beach to his clothes.

She was there, watching him. Bridget Egan, with a stone in her hand.

It shouldn't have died, she said, throwing the stone at the whale. By her feet, a pile of pebbles. She picked up another and threw it, wiping her face with the back of her hand. She stopped. And looked at Tommy. Her eyes sliding down to his underpants.

He turned his back on her. Grabbed his vest and dried himself. Bridget was in his class but came on the bus. Her father worked the trawlers. He knew they lived near Carna. He pulled on his clothes and turned to face her, screwing the damp vest in a ball.

'I've seen you here before,' she said.

'You shouldn't be doing that,' he said.

'Spying on you?'

'Throwing stones.'

Bridget shrugged.

Tommy stuffed the vest in his pocket. 'Why aren't you at school?' he asked.

'Because of the whale. Mammie said I should make a shrine for it. So as I won't feel sad. But you can't change sad.'

Bridget pushed her foot through the pile of stones. She gave Tommy a sideways look.

'Your sister was washed off the pier. In the spring tide. You were with her.'

He turned to the whale. Counted the pleats in its long white throat.

'Daddie says it wasn't your fault. Says it was the full moon.'

Tommy had blamed so many things.

'Look!' Bridget shouted, her arm wavering in the wind as she pointed out to sea. 'Can you see them? Seals!'

Tommy saw the three dark heads appear and disappear. He'd made up a story for Maeve, that special Sunday. He'd forgotten till now.

He looked at the small brave heads, bobbing up and down in the waves. It had been a lovely story.

'Maeve's with the mermaids,' he said.

'That's nice,' said Bridget. 'I'd like to go there, when my time comes. My Gran's in the cemetery. It's awful sad there. The flowers, they're all plastic.'

She ground her toe into the sand, dragging the circle wider and wider. Her foot stopped. She looked at him.

'I knew you'd come today. I told Mammie you would. She said to ask you up. For your dinner. She says you're always welcome. Do you like sausages?'

Tommy picked up his shoes and followed her across the sand.

The Slipper
Jenny Morris

The woman died. The man grieved. After nine days he began to look for another wife.

She was easy to find. A young widow who had recently moved to a nearby village caught his eye on the bus.

More difficult to deal with was the man's only daughter, Sindy, Sin for short, who was plain, indulged and discontented. The sun really fell out of the sky for her on the day her mother died. Sin became more pale and pouting and refused even to attempt to tie up her own laces.

Her father swiftly courted and married the widow. He was very content.

The widow was as wise as she was beautiful. Her long ebony hair hung in a gleaming plait down her back and her dark eyes glowed with kindness. She had two small daughters of her own who had inherited her attractive appearance and compassionate nature. All three tried to please resentful Sin, but to no avail. The stepmother did her best for the family, cooking, cleaning and mending, but in those days there were many troubles.

Spiteful Sin was a sort of ugly duckling who would never learn swanlike behaviour. She made sure that she had an easy life, never having to do any domestic task, simply refusing to lift a finger for anyone else. The Beautiful Sisters were pleased to be able to help their mother, but in time they gradually fell under the malign influence of their stepsister and learned that self-interest has its own reward.

Sin demanded all her father's affection, time and money.

'I'm your only true daughter. Your only flesh and blood, after all,' she said. But her jealousy was abruptly terminated one day when he suffered a heart attack and died. Life changed for her and she missed him for the attention he'd given her.

The stepmother was left in a state of unenviable penury, with three girls to bring up. She worked for them, leaving the house before dawn to travel a long distance to a tedious factory job in the city. She returned late, exhausted, in her well-worn black widow's coat, then cleaned and baked far into the night.

Sin rejected everything that her stepmother did for the family, all her high standards of care and behaviour. She taught the Beautiful

Sisters to scoff at their mother's old-fashioned ideals and work ethics. The woman had hardly time to think herself unhappy, as all her energies were devoted to making a proper job of bringing up the girls on a tiny income. It seemed to her to be always winter, and her dark hair became increasingly touched by frost.

Her prince was coming, though, in the guise of a shy local corner shop assistant who first admired her good looks from afar, then fell passionately in love with her. But he was a tongue-tied young man who only knew how to please her with past-their-sell-by-date items. It would have taken more than pots of slimming yoghurt, however, to get under the defences of Sin, who had no intention of allowing any man to bring happiness to her stepmother.

Sin waylaid him at the garden gate.

'She doesn't want to see you.' Or, 'She's gone out.' Or, 'She can't stand your stale and rotten stuff.' Or just, 'Get lost.'

But the following week Sin flirted with him, peeping up at him under her pale lashes, blowing him kisses, winding her arm around his hips as he stood, upset and blinking on the path.

The stepmother called to him from an upstairs window, and he stumbled into the house, Sin giggling behind him.

'Whatever's the matter with that girl?' he muttered to the woman, uneasily stroking his fair hair.

'She's just growing up. Feeling her way. Be kind.'

But the courtship was being ruined by Sin's behaviour.

The next Sunday when he called she was dressed up in a new lilac frock and had bows in her hair. She sat on the stone steps and blocked his entrance, crossing and uncrossing her white-socked legs. Her unattractive, plump, rabbity face seemed to fill his vision. Watching him attentively, she stroked her knees.

'What do you want, Sin?' he asked gruffly, fearfully, backing away.

'Am I pretty?'

'Well... I expect so.'

But the pause was too long. She lost her temper. 'You are ugly. Foul. With a face like a horrible fungus. And my stepmother thinks so too. We all hate you.'

She slammed into the house, leaving him unsettled outside. It was all too much trouble going there. He decided to leave for good, back to the safe, cold shop cellar that smelled of pickles and loneliness.

The stepmother was hardly conscious of her loss, for by now she spent all her spare time sewing dresses for the girls and earning the money to pay for their dancing lessons. She would never dance again, she knew, as each night she sat by the dying embers of the fire and felt herself growing older.

Time passed and the dark, rosy-cheeked Beautiful Sisters grew up and were quickly married to handsome bachelors, who passed by, saw them, and carried them off triumphantly.

Sin was left behind, plain and cross. She took to wandering about the city, looking for trouble, buying expensive fripperies with her stepmother's money, and coming home to lie on her bed and issue orders. She insisted on having cosmetic surgery to create a retroussé nose from its original potato shape. Not content with that, next she had huge breast implants. Still no-one seemed interested.

She thought about the grocer's assistant again. With her new assets she could possibly snare him and benefit herself while inflicting yet more hurt on her stepmother.

After years of quietly labouring with groceries, the fair haired man had inherited the small business and saved a considerable amount of money.

Sin, dressed in skimpy, provocative clothes, and carrying large bottles of brandy, began visiting him at night. She teased and tormented him, insisting that he break open a new stock of shop candles, light them and turn off the electricity.

It was true, he thought, that she looked better by candlelight, her cross expression softened, her lumps and bumps smoothed away. He fell under the spell of her unrealistic figure. He drank more than was good for him. He refused to let himself think of her lovely, gentle stepmother. I'm a useless coward, he thought, and stroked Sin's lazy, naked arm.

'Look what I've got,' she snickered, and lay down on his floor.

He sighed. There was no escape.

'I love you. Do you love me?' She was relentless.

His chin was bristly to her. It reminded her of her father, so long ago. She liked it. But he was too hesitant, too unsure of himself, too apologetic.

She thought pregnancy would be the answer. There could be no refusal. She caressed his toes. She admired his taste in ties. She smiled a lot to herself.

Her stepmother was pleased that Sin seemed happier, that she had an unknown project, that she was out a great deal.

Each evening in the mirror Sin puckered her lips and sprayed herself with scent. After she had gone, the older woman stood in the cloud of perfume and sighed. My eyes are wearing out, she thought, I look permanently tired.

Sin broke her important news to the grocer. Aghast, he tried to control his expression.

'You're quite sure?'

'Quite.'

Later they walked out to choose an engagement ring.

The cold white stone reflected the glitter in Sin's eyes. 'Let's go and tell my stepmother right now!'

He paled and said he had to get back to work. All birds had stopped singing and the sky had dulled.

But his fiancée was insistent, and together they entered the house and let the stepmother make them tea.

After he had seen his former love's look of anguish on being told the glad tidings, he, for once, asserted himself and declared that he and Sin were moving away and marrying in a different town.

After the wedding, it seemed there was no longer any pregnancy. Sin lay on her new leather sofa a great deal, reading magazines and drinking large quantities of gin. Her husband bought her a dog, but she refused to take it for walks.

The stepmother finally retired. Her pension was small. She was lonely. She didn't eat properly; she became very thin; she imagined things. She sometimes sang to herself behind her net curtains. She sometimes turned the gas taps on and forgot to light the gas. Her neighbours were concerned. Sin and the Beautiful Sisters were summoned.

'What shall we do with her?'

'She's senile. She isn't fit to be on her own.' Sin's voice was sharp and emphatic. 'But she can't live with us.'

'Why not? You have plenty of room.'

'You know she's always fancied the grocer. Awful when she can't be trusted with your own husband.'

'That's not true, surely?'

But the Beautiful Sisters were less compassionate now and involved with their own families.

'There's no question of her coming abroad with us. She couldn't understand our cleaning woman.'

'I'm a full time career woman. There would be no-one to care for her at our house.'

They stared at each other for a long moment. Then Sin, throwing a cushion at her bony dog for no apparent reason, said firmly, 'She must go in a home. Some of these places are palaces.'

And so it happened.

But the home, chosen by Sin, was unlike any home that the

stepmother had ever known. It was more of a surrealist vista where vacant-eyed, drugged ancients existed like rows of shrivelled beans awaiting the plough. The days stretched out endlessly.

The Beautiful Sisters and Sin fell upon the stepmother's possessions without asking her permission. Like wolves they divided the spoils and carried them off.

The Beautiful Sisters spent the rest of their lives in harmony, occasionally spoiled by moments of remorse. Not Sin. She took to the bottle seriously, becoming increasingly more spendthrift and wrathful towards her husband.

One morning, badly hung-over, she rose late at the sound of the milkman's ring. She flung herself into her flowing dressing gown and huffled onto the landing.

The dog had just retrieved one of the grocer's slippers from under the bed and was intent on attacking it on the stairs.

'Push off!' she shouted, kicking him violently.

Yelping, he dropped the slipper and fled.

It was a large, worn, brown piece of footwear, the same colour as the stair carpet. Sin never saw it on the second step. Putting her podgy foot into it, she slid and hurtled down the stairs with an almighty crash. She broke her neck instantly.

The milkman peered through the letterbox and opening the unlocked door, quickly summoned an ambulance.

The grocer came home and was not surprised at anything he saw. He shed no tears.

After Sin's cremation, he decided to rescue the stepmother he had always loved. He carried her away from the home in triumph, back to his own home and faithful dog.

She was touched to see the fuss he was able to make of her at last, and wept tears of joy. From that moment on she was properly cared for. Undrugged, on a healthy diet and a great deal of affection, she recovered her memory and muddled wits. To her surprise, she learned to laugh again. Each evening she and her former suitor played chess with good humour and serenity. It was a storybook ending.

Homecoming
Piers Blaikie

George Sibbald ventured out of his stifling cabin of the ship which he had shared with two other merchants for 125 days and stood in the shade, dressed in britches and an unbuttoned white shirt. Beads of perspiration had already appeared at the opening of his collar where a ginger tuft of hair sprouted upwards towards his chin.

He was bored – uplifting tomes and religious texts had palled and his mind fell again to the prospect of making money. Yes, he was anxious to start his commercial business in Calcutta as soon as he could. He would go to the Offices of the East India Company to look up an old Scots compatriot who had done him favours during his last visit.

'Let me hope that the Good Lord will have preserved his life, at least,' he thought, eyes cast to the heavens, which offered on this occasion little to lift the spirits. His attention wandered to thinking how many more of his small circle of fellow traders and congenial friends in Calcutta would have succumbed to pestilence since his last trip eighteen months ago. He recalled that one young man had died on the voyage and had to be buried at sea. Those with downcast eyes at the service were also mulling over the chances of the death being caused by cholera and how it might already have spread to claim other passengers and crew alike. Rumours abounded but no one else had died. His own thoughts had taken an anxious turn, but to seek out the company of his missionary fellow passengers for moral stiffening did not appeal.

The ship was being taken by the flood tide into the outer reaches of the Hooghly delta. A smudge of mangrove trees on the horizon gave a lift to the ship's company. A faint but palpable smell of wet mud and smoke from dung fires and of sun-drying fish marked the border of land and ocean – the land so impatiently longed for after the long sea passage. Arrival was now imminent but when the low-lying coastline first became visible, it lay uninviting with intimations of pestilence, dark foreign faces and moral benightedness. As George had written to his brother after his previous visit:

This is a land of Moral Darkness, where idolatry in its worst form as described in the Bible prevails. Some may have conjured up favoured tales of innocence and peace among the Hindoos, but the very reverse is the case. The first chapter of the Epistle to the Romans is a faithful description of the people in general, and even among their own caste no one thinks of another as his neighbour. A total lack of confidence prevails, every man seems only to live for himself and is careless of all besides.

To clear his mind he decided to take a short walk towards the bows of the ship, but a sense of diffuse outrage at the state of humankind here in Bengal persisted as he looked over the taffrail into the brown muddy water. It was then he saw a partly burnt corpse floating down the river. A skull, blackened, its shape still recognisable, gobbets of fat and skin adhering to yellowed bones, some pieces of unburnt wood under the body were floating down the river. It bobbed, curiously alive, even playful, under the bow. During his previous visit, he had learnt of the practice of sati in which widows were burnt alive on the pyre of their dead husband, but he had never actually seen its physical residue. He gagged, crossed himself and returned to the refuge of the saloon. He longed for the safe haven of the residential quarters for employees of the Company where he could relax among people of his own kith and kin.

By the late afternoon the ship had been moored at the Company's landing stages and warehouses which lined the muddy banks of the Hooghly. Upon disembarking, familiar smells enveloped him – cow dung from large numbers of zebu cattle that wandered across the dusty tracks and piles of rotting vegetable matter. A mild but pervasive distaste of the inhabitants of the city and a fear of infection assailed him. His contact with Bengalis was limited to traders with networks of supply of cotton and jute in the interior. Of Indian women he knew nothing but he had heard that they were supplied to the soldiers and that some of the more well-to-do officials of the company lived with Indian mistresses.

During his visits to Calcutta he was billeted in a small bungalow belonging to a Mr Donald Logie, a senior official of the East India Company, who had also become a friend. It was situated in the extensive gardens of a larger house built in the Palladian style where Mr Logie lived and George was usually invited to dinner there. It was helpful that his landlord was also Scots, even if he was of a less prudent and religious nature. Dinner was held in a large gloomy dining room set about with portraits of worthy officers of the Company. Silver decanters, candelabra and ornaments glinted from its darker recesses.

Madeira and port flowed freely at the dinner table that night and His Majesty George IV's health was formally drunk at the end of the meal. After a few minutes the lady of the house withdrew and left the men to discuss the Company's business, and their views on India and its inhabitants. On this occasion George was introduced to a guest whom he had not met before, a Mr Percival Arkright. He was slight, pale-faced, neatly dressed, as rapid in eye movement as in speech and judging from his accent a highly educated Englishman.

After dinner, talk turned as usual to business, the dealings of the company and their views of the native population. George was confused by Mr Arkright's deftly delivered points of view on the policies of the Company. He seemed to favour the reforms of Lord William Bentick to sweep away the corruption and bloated salaries of Company officials. He sympathised with the progressive educational and social policies which were currently being made. So far, George was able to nod in agreement, especially as the visitor obviously thought highly of the political philosophy of John Stuart Mill (a fellow Scot). The visitor seemed less than enthusiastic about Bentick's sympathies with evangelical Christian missionaries, and George started to clear his throat in muted disagreement. Then the visitor, whom George was beginning to mark down as a dangerous liberal and a Whig, started to tell the after dinner company about some British soldiers and adventurers who had joined the courts of the still independent Muslim states in southern India as advisors, soldiers and liaison officers.

'What's more,' he explained, warming to his theme, 'many of them have taken Muslim women as their wives – quite openly and with the approval of the rulers. They have to agree to be circumcised before the marriage ceremony' (at this point Mr. Arkright's eye gave a precautionary glance to the door to be sure no lady had heard this), 'and the children of these unions are brought up as Muslims. Indeed, many of our fellow countrymen can speak fluent Urdu.'

His host and other dinner guests were rather more inclined to be intrigued and interested in the account than to make a moral judgement on it. George's initial reaction was one of horror at the triple sins of lust, miscegenation and the abandonment of Christian faith. He tried to insert his disapproval into the enthusiastic explanations of the visitor, but without much effect. He left the proceedings after giving a curt excuse of having to rise early next day. Strolling back to his bungalow, he felt his moral outrage being compromised by the same lurid curiosity and implicit acceptance shown by the dinner guests. After all, these men were not behaving as the common soldiers and libertines living here in Calcutta who were known to keep mistresses. These Muslim converts had shown respect to both the women and the customs of the day – they were not, by the standards of any faith, living in sin. George felt these contrary currents of emancipation and sin swirl around him as he stepped onto the verandah of his bungalow.

Later in the week, George had a full day's work at the Head Office of the Company trying to secure an advantageous price for consignments of cotton and jute. He was tired, but the evening was cool, so he took the unprecedented decision to forsake the buggy which had come to take him home and take a shortcut which skirted the native quarter just outside the civil lines. As he was walking close to a large set of buildings built around a courtyard, he noticed with distaste that the walls of the Hindu temple were encrusted with idolatrous statues. He hastily averted his eye. But he could not avert his ear, which picked up the sound of a woman's voice singing. It seemed to him to be a hymn. He heard a number of plaintive and repeated musical phrases, ending in a shudder of three short notes. A small dismissive shake of his head, as if disposing of an insect in his ear, was not enough to stop his consciousness being flooded in a bright light of calm and joy. That it was unbidden, unexplained and unearned alarmed him. He tried to evoke his ready prejudice against any religious songs that differed from the Low Church plainsong hymns sung in his parish in Scotland, but righteous anger simply would not come. He shook his head again but this time in resignation and bafflement. He knew a seed had been planted within him.

He arrived back at the bungalow in pensive mood, changed into fresh britches and tunic and came into dinner. He was met by Donald Logie on the verandah, who briefly greeted him and then told him of the sudden deaths from fever of not one but two of the junior clerks of the Company. George knew well that life for the European colony was precarious. While the news of these deaths came as no surprise, it reminded him again of his own mortality, for the preservation from which every night he gave thanks to God. Dinner was a subdued occasion; the garrulous new visitor had left and no royal toast was drunk. After Mrs Logie had left the table, the men fell to glum small talk that did not last. They arose from the dining table, bid each other 'good night' and went to bed.

George awoke suddenly. It was dark. Immediately he heard again in his mind the descending song of prayer with its shudder of short notes as he had heard at the temple earlier that day and felt the same joy, the emancipation from worldly worries and the falling away of all preoccupations that assailed him. An instant later he realised he was in the grip of a wild fever. He was bathed in sweat and gasping for breath. He tried to fight his way out of bed to reach fresh air, became entangled in the mosquito net and fell off the bed. The floor came up and smacked him hard on the forehead and nose. He lay face down on the floor with his torso still on the bed, bound tightly in the white shroud of the net. His breath bubbled through his bleeding nose. He groped feebly towards fresh air and prayer.

'Oh Lord our Heavenly Father, almighty and everlasting God, who hast safely brought us to the beginning of this day' – here he stopped, gasping for air and the rest of the prayer that had momentarily eluded him – 'defend us in the same with thy mighty power; and grant that this day we fall into no sin, neither run into any kind of danger.' Then, at the point of finishing his prayer, she burst upon his mind's eye. She, the woman who sang the Hindu prayer whom he had heard earlier in the day – even although he had never actually seen her then. When he beheld her at that moment, he knew it was her. She stopped singing, lips slightly parted. Then she composed herself and looked at George, as if gently appraising him. He held every tiny detail of her in breathless wonderment, her smooth wheaten complexion, luminous brown eyes and her smile for him – not the alluring smile of desire but one sharing a sublime and secret joke with him. She seemed to be saying, 'Don't you know our blessed secret, don't you want to know what it is?' Then she swayed slightly to one side to reveal a perfect little boy of four or five years old, who had been standing behind her. He recognised him immediately – *their* boy, *their* flesh and blood. He exulted in her and in their son as he had never exulted in anyone before, even in the days when he was first married and in the birth of his own children back home in Melrose long ago.

He knew then he had fallen into sin, even if only in thought. Unaccountably joyful but threatened by death, he could explain these feelings only as a punishment for hearing and being overtaken by heathen song, for apparently having married a non-Christian and committing bigamy, even if only in his imagination. All these sins had brought forth a call to judgement from his God and Maker. Again he tried to pray, but the Third Collect for Grace eluded him, and the notes of the devotional song of the temple wove in and out of the austere words of Presbyterian prayer like a garland of summer jasmine. Those notes and her face floated between him and his Maker with feelings of the lightness and joy of being. Thoughts of death and judgement faded away.

He must have slept. He woke to hear the muezzin calling the

faithful to prayer as it came with the rising of the sun, then a little later the tinkling of bells calling Hindus to their temples. He managed to disentangle himself from the mosquito net and lie back on the bed still soaked in sweat, shuddering in spasms every few minutes. He lay still for another long period until he was awoken by the noise of a large black crow pecking at the window. He caught its inquisitive amber eye looking at him through the glass. Then he knew the crisis was past and he would survive. But no longer in the world he had known.

Not Much to Tell
Sally Alexander

It was answers Annie said she wanted. What the questions were was never clear. She talked a lot about responsibility. He was her father, after all; he should want to be a part of her life, didn't I agree? I said I supposed I did. I was just happy that she was talking; that she got up in the morning, washed and dressed herself. The day she hired the private detective was the first day she'd worn lipstick for three months. She sat at the breakfast table with her face painted and her hair combed, ordering piles of paper. 'We're really making progress,' she told me.

It was years ago, before we were married, when Annie first told me about her family situation. She had never met her father; her parent's relationship had fallen apart before her mother discovered that she was pregnant. Her father had been informed of the birth and had sent a bunch of crushed carnations to her in the hospital, along with a money order for fifty pounds.

'Quite a lot of money in those days,' Annie had said.

'And you've never been curious? You've never wanted to find him?'

'No. He's got nothing to do with me really, has he? He's just a name on my birth certificate.'

Even after her mother died and we were clearing out the bungalow, it was me who convinced Annie to keep the box of letters and old photographs labelled 'Jack Harwood'. She'd been all for tipping it into the skip with the other junk that we couldn't find a place for in our house. I said that if we had children some day, they might like to know where they came from. She thought that we would be enough. Jack Harwood. She never called him that; she never called him Dad or Father either; back then he was merely 'the biological factor'. Recently, she'd been referring to him as Pa.

It's taken time to track him down and most of our money. Private detectives don't come cheap and we've not had as much cash to play with since Annie stopped working. In the end I took a weekend job driving a taxi to help pay the bills. I didn't mind, it was nice to get out of the house; forget about everything for a while. Annie wanted me to put a flyer up in the cab: *Have you seen Jack Harwood?* but I told her that my boss wouldn't like it. In truth, I never asked him. I just wanted to keep things separate. We both need our different escapes.

There have been a lot of false leads; trails of addresses that have run cold. Jack has proved a hard man to track down. Annie must have been to every house and flat that her father has rented in the past thirty-five years. Every one but the last. She knocks on doors and asks if she can look around; mostly people let her in. She has a process, she tells me: living-room first; then bedroom, bathroom and finally the kitchen. She asks whoever's living there if the walls have been painted or if they've had new units installed; she notes down stains on the work surfaces and views from the windows; she has a special notebook, like a reporter's, that she bought for the purpose. After she's finished with the house, she visits the local shops and asks if anyone remembers her father. The private detective will have already covered this ground, but she likes to go herself. She says that it gives her a sense of her father; this way it's like she's already met him; like they've already caught up on lost time.

When the private detective phoned to say that he'd found Jack, Annie was very quiet. She wrote down the telephone number and address that he gave her and then sat staring at it.

'You don't have to contact him if you don't want to. It's OK if you've changed your mind.'

'It's not that,' she said, still staring at the paper. 'It's just that I don't think I can phone him. I want to *see* him. The first time we meet, I want to do it properly.'

In the end I made the call. He answered on the third ring, reciting the number I'd just dialled, like they do in old movies. A strong male voice. I explained who I was and told him that my wife had been trying to find him for some time; she was the daughter of Diana Gregory. Annie watched me from across the kitchen, her hands folded in her lap. She had written out a list of things I was to say, marking each point with a little star. As I spoke, she mouthed the prepared sentences, staring at the receiver in my hand. She looked very pale. Jack Harwood took my call in a businesslike fashion; he asked if this was anything to do with money; he'd offered to help, but Diana had written to him and said that she was able to support the child. He was an old man now and a pension didn't go far. I told him this was nothing to do with money; my wife merely wanted to get in contact with her father; was there the possibility that they could meet?

He came to lunch today. Annie spent the morning fussing with sofa cushions and flowers; she changed her clothes twice, finally settling on a pale blue suit that she'd bought for her first week back at work, but never worn. I'd brought in fresh rolls and made a salad. We waited in the living-room, watching the window.

When the doorbell rang, we stared at one another. I got up, but she grabbed my arm.

'I don't know if I can do this.'

'Just wait here. I'll get the door and bring him through to you.'

I left her on the sofa, picking at the fold in her skirt, and found Jack trying the door handle.

'Ah, there you are. Wasn't sure if you heard me,' he said, stepping back.

He was a short man, grey hair smoothed back over a ruddy scalp, broken veins across his nose and under his eyes, very blue eyes. Annie's eyes are brown. I invited him in and held the door as he passed into the hall. He smelt of charity shops and cigarettes, like someone's grandfather.

Annie stood up as we entered the living room. Her heel caught in the carpet and she tottered towards us; Jack put out his arms as if to catch her and they stood facing, each unsure how to greet the other. It was Jack who broke the silence.

'You must be my daughter, then.' He chuckled and took hold of her hand. 'Pleasure to meet you at last, I must say. But better late than never, as my mother always said.'

'Yes,' was all that Annie found to say. She looked confused. Finally, with a weak kind of smile, she sat back down on the sofa.

I left them and went into the kitchen to fetch a bottle of wine. The unfamiliar rumble of Jack's voice followed me through and I wondered how long it had been since anyone had spoken loudly in this house. Apart from the daily updates in the search for Pa, Annie and I hardly spoke a word.

When I came back into the room I saw that Jack had seated himself next to Annie on the sofa. He'd pulled a leather tobacco pouch from his pocket and Annie was watching his hands as he rolled a stout cigarette.

'Ah, there you are,' he said again, looking up at me. 'You don't mind this do you? Filthy habit I know, but one of life's great pleasures all the same.'

He pinched some stray tobacco from the end of the cigarette and looked about for an ashtray. I tipped the glass beads out of one of Annie's little decorative plates and handed it to him.

'Thank you. Oh, and wine too. Bit early for me, but I wouldn't mind a small one.' He took his glass and settled back against the sofa cushions. 'Lovely place you have here. I was saying to Ann, I've always liked these new builds. Nice and clean.'

Jack lit his cigarette and exhaled loudly. The smell of smoke filled the room, overpowering the perfume of the lilacs carefully arranged on the coffee table. I watched the smoke drift and thought of it making its way through our nice clean house, up the stairs and into the waiting bedrooms, like an intruder. The smell will linger. Days later, long after this man is gone, after we've opened windows and flushed the rooms with clean air, we will stumble into the whiff of stale smoke; a souvenir of Jack's visit.

'I was sorry to hear about Di. Not that we'd kept in touch, but there was always a card at Christmas to my Mum and Dad. She was like that. Nice woman. What took her in the end?'

'Cancer,' Annie said. She was staring at her wine glass now, rotating the stem slowly between her fingers. 'Five years ago.'

'Five years! Well, as I say we weren't really in touch. I don't suppose she told you much about me?'

'Not much.'

'Well there's not much to tell, if you want the truth of it. We weren't together that long. I had lots of girlfriends back then and a fair few of them were careless. Your Mum was one of the good ones though. Yes, I've always kept a soft spot for Di. She never called me up asking for money or giving me lectures about what I should or shouldn't be doing. No, she minded her business, did Di. My Dad always said I should have married her.'

'Are you married?' I asked.

'No. Never went in for marriage myself. Thought about it once or twice, but they never seemed to be the right girl. I'm happy enough on my own – happier even – and I've got my daughters, of course.'

'So you have other children?' I looked across at Annie, but she was still turning her wine glass, her eyes fixed on the swilling liquid.

'Oh yes. I was telling her while you were out there getting the drinks. This is my third stop like this one. Three lovely girls. Sue and Lizzie, those are my other two. Tracked me down, like you did. Wait, I think I've got some pictures somewhere.'

He set his wine glass down on the coffee table and reached into an inside pocket of his jacket. He handed me three photographs.

'Your sisters, these are,' he said, with a nod at Annie. 'That dark one, that's Lizzie. She's a bit of a high-flyer in computers. Got her own flat in London and always jetting off somewhere new. She's a lovely looking girl, isn't she? Must get that from me, because her mother was nothing to look at. She's been trying to get me on to using that Internet stuff, says it'll be better for us keeping in touch. I don't know what's wrong with a letter or a phone call now and then, but she's a busy girl. I suppose she doesn't get much time.

'Now that's Sue and her husband Jeremy. He's a nice bloke. Sue's my homemaker; that other picture there is of her three. Charlotte, Harry and Jack. Can you believe that? Called her boy after me before she even knew me. I found out about her a couple of years back and they had me round for Christmas. Her mother was off on some cruise, so it was all right my being there. They love their Grandpa Jack, those three. Drew me pictures. Just some nonsense in crayon, but I put them up on the wall when I got back. You two got any kids?'

I passed the photographs to Annie. Three smiling blonde-haired children shone in her pale blue lap. Jack looked from me to her, his cigarette end between his lips.

'We had a son,' Annie said. 'Peter.'

'Shame. I'm always hoping for another Jack. Still, you never know, I might have a son out there somewhere. I've always fancied having a boy, to carry on the family name and all that.

'Here love, you know you don't look well at all. Are you all right? Take that glass off her before it goes everywhere.'

Annie got to her feet and stood awkwardly in the space between the sofa and the coffee table.

'I'm afraid there's been a mistake,' she said. 'I'm afraid that you'll have to leave now.'

I managed to get Jack out of the living room and into the hallway without too much fuss.

'I'm sorry about this,' I told him. 'It's just that this is a difficult time.'

'Don't worry about me, son. It's a shock for the girl, seeing her father after all these years. It's to be expected. And I did say, didn't I, that it's never a good idea to be drinking this early in the day, especially with a scrap of a thing like that. I mean to say, those clothes are hanging off her. It might be an idea to get her to the doctor's. I'm healthy as an ox, but after her mother and all that. You never know with these things.'

We were at the door when he paused again.

'Not one for pictures are you? I notice these things. Not even a snap of your little one. It's just that I wondered if I could trouble you for a couple of photos of Ann and the boy. It's a silly thing, but I like to have them by me. Just one nice photo to go in with the others. Then I can keep the family together.'

58

After he'd gone, I went back. The bay window was open and Jack's ashtray and glass were missing. I refilled my glass and sat down. As the room cooled, I listened to the murmur of distant traffic. Much later, Annie joined me. She'd scrubbed her face and changed into jeans and a sweatshirt.

'He wasn't right,' she said at last. 'I don't know who that man was, but he wasn't Pa.'

Loss
Martin Drummond

When Hitler went into Poland, Nicholas d'Aubigny joined his late father's regiment. His shyness didn't matter in the army, and the friends he made in North Africa were the closest of his life. He survived a stomach wound on D-Day and finished the war a captain, but did not find the transition to civilian life easy. With his war service grant he read Classics at Christchurch, got a well-deserved third, and finally floundered into banking. There his colleagues found him unsociable, and worse, subject to outbursts of sudden rage triggered by apparently minor frustrations.

His mother continued to manage the family estate in Hampshire. Robertswell Hall, lying in a fold of the Downs, was arranged around three sides of a paved courtyard, parkland falling away down to the river and good shooting in the woods above. There Nicholas enjoyed the only social life he knew when his mother invited her friends and neighbours to dine. One of these had a daughter, Elisabeth, like him a little shy and formal, and as soon as the slightest attachment between them was discernible their parents arranged that they should meet more frequently. It worked; they married. More remarkably, they were happy. She admired his intellect, he her undoubted beauty, and neither believed that they would ever be lonely again.

Soon after marrying, Nicholas distinguished himself by striking an office clerk, and while his seniors were considering his future, or lack of it, his mother suggested he assume management of the estate. He left the bank. In time Elisabeth allied herself with the old lady to form a quietly competent duo capable of managing everything, including Nicholas, whose sense of belonging depended on the occasional requests made of him. Most of his time was spent in the library reading ancient history, in fine weather sitting outside the French windows, his dog lying at his side.

When their son Matthew was born, Elisabeth engaged a nanny. Nicholas disliked babies, and ignored the child until he was about five. Then one afternoon an expedition of the womenfolk obliged the father to look after his son for a few hours.

'What are you reading, Daddy?'

'Herodotus.'

'What's that?'

Nicholas snorted, paused, and then began to tell the little boy the old story of Persian arrogance and Greek defiance, of Marathon and of Salamis. He told it well, and the boy listened intently. Next day he came back, and his father told him of Alexander, then Hannibal.

They took to walking together around the estate, and Matthew would ride alone with his father in the front seat of the old Jaguar, eagerly learning about cars. One morning the two grandmothers observed father and son leaning over an engine, Matthew watching as Nicholas adjusted the carburettor.

'They seem to be great chums,' said the visitor.

'Very much so,' said Nicholas's mother. 'Matthew wants to be a soldier like his daddy.'

When the time came for his son to board at Winchester, Nicholas realised that he would miss him, and Elisabeth agreed that the local grammar school would be just as satisfactory. So it proved; the boy excelled in all examinations. Nicholas decided that he should go to Oxford, perhaps to read History. Matthew chose English at Warwick. Not really a university, thought his father; still, good enough for Sandhurst.

His son became interested in film and after graduation joined an action vehicle company.

'What's that?' demanded Nicholas.

'Car chases, mostly,' said Matthew. Not a real job, thought his father, won't last.

Matthew brought his girlfriend home, Elaine, a set designer. She regarded Nicholas with as much interest as a goldfish might give a rock. Not the girl for my boy, thought Nicholas, won't last.

'What do you think of Elaine?' Elisabeth asked her husband.

'Ice maiden,' he replied. 'Don't like her.'

His wife studied her nails and said nothing.

Matthew developed the lazy habit of leaving his car outside the library instead of driving it round to the garage. Nicholas's indulgence finally snapped when Elaine parked it a yard from his French windows with the engine running. He stepped briskly from the door: 'Excuse me.' His hostile tone was a shock to the girl. 'Be so good as to take your car to the garage.'

Flustered, she engaged the wrong gear and jerked forward instead of reversing. The old dog dozing on the stone flags had his skull crushed without even waking. Nicholas, frighteningly pale, didn't say a word, but turned back into the house, and she heard him shout for his son.

A few moments later Matthew emerged.

'What's happened?'

'I seem to have run over the dog. Not my fault.'

'Oh my God! Poor Nemo! But come and make up with Dad. He's terribly upset.'

They went back inside. Nicholas was standing in a corner of the library fiddling with the tassel of a curtain.

'I'm sorry about the dog, Mr d'Aubigny. I didn't know... I didn't mean... well, it was quite an old dog wasn't it? A Labrador? I'll buy you a new one.'

He started towards her hissing 'Out! Out! Out!', and Matthew bundled her through the door.

'Oh dear. I think we'd better go and see Mummy.'

Elisabeth was sewing in her upstairs room and listened gravely.

'I shall speak with him,' she said. 'I think it would be better not to mention the matter again. We will have dinner together as usual. Do please take care to be absolutely civil.'

'Don't worry,' said Matthew to Elaine. 'It'll blow over.'

But their studied manners at dinner made the atmosphere worse, and at last Elaine could stand it no longer.

'Mr d'Aubigny, believe me, I am truly sorry about your dog. I'm not a dog person myself, but I do understand how much you will miss it.'

Elisabeth froze. Nicholas finished chewing for fully ten seconds and leaned forwards.

'It? It? She! Had her fourteen years. Don't even have a pup of hers now. But pray do not concern yourself,' he smiled offensively at the young woman: 'A common bitch can be found anywhere.'

Elaine rose and left the room. After a moment's hesitation Matthew followed. Three minutes later a car door slammed and his parents heard the vehicle leave.

'I wish you could have just accepted her apology, Nicholas,' said his wife.

'Why should I accept anything from that cold fish. The sooner Matthew gets rid of her the better, and if I've brought that day any closer then I'm glad.'

'My dear, rudeness is always a mistake. I'm afraid he likes her.'

At Christmas Matthew and Elaine were still together, and Nicholas reluctantly conceded that they could both be invited to Robertswell.

Elisabeth rang her son, then went down to the library.

'Matthew said they will come provided that you apologise to Elaine.'

'Why on earth should I?'

'He says you called her a bitch.'

'Rubbish! You were there. Tell him he's mistaken.'

And Matthew spent his first Christmas away from home.

The following June he called his mother in great excitement. He'd been offered work on a Hollywood blockbuster with a lavish budget for action vehicles, was off to California at the end of the month with Elaine.

'You must come and see us before you go.'

'Of course.' But cheap flights and their hectic departure schedule prevented it.

Letters came. Matthew was doing well. One day the parents received the news both secretly feared; he intended to marry Elaine, in California, probably that summer. Elisabeth remonstrated with her son on the telephone.

'Mum, all our friends are in L.A.'

'But a wedding is a family affair. What about Elaine's parents?'

'They're already out here. We're going to come back at Christmas.'

Elisabeth resigned herself to travelling. Nicholas refused.

'Why should I fly halfway round the world to celebrate that harpy getting her claws into my son?'

'Because he is your son, and that's what he's chosen. Do try to be generous, Nicholas.'

While he was thinking it over, his mother was diagnosed with nephritis, providing all the excuse he needed. And more; by the time Elisabeth returned from California the old lady was dead. Matthew could not come to his grandmother's funeral. Nicholas stood impassive at the damp graveside, as Elisabeth sobbed quietly for both of them.

At Christmas the newlyweds did not return to England because Elaine was heavily pregnant.

'You see?' said Nicholas. 'She trapped him.'

'Young people do not consider themselves trapped by such things these days', said his wife. 'And in any case, it was March when they decided to get married.'

In the spring Elisabeth wanted to go to California to see her

63

grandson.

'All that way to see a baby?' asked Nicholas.

'Of course. And Matthew. Whom you have not seen for three years.'

'I am told that Los Angeles is a horrible place. Let him come here.'

She returned with an armful of photographs, all featuring baby Dominic held by one or other beaming parent in front of various landmarks.

'They say they want to come back this Christmas, but there's some difficulty. It depends on Matthew's new boss, who does seem to be an unpleasant person.'

That autumn Elisabeth had a stroke. She lay in bed with one half of her face drooping horribly, barely articulate. Nicholas spent hours every day reading the newspaper to her and stroking her hand. He telephoned Matthew.

'Your mother's very ill. She wants to see you.'

'I want to see her, Dad, but Elaine and I are both working flat out on this film. And childcare is hell.'

'What about Christmas?'

'Christmas! We get two days off and Elaine won't want me charging off to Europe.'

'Matthew, anything could happen.'

The sombre 'anything' hung between them.

'I'll have to discuss it with Elaine.'

'I think it would be better if you made up your mind and simply informed her of your decision.'

Matthew did not come, and in mid-January a second stroke killed Elisabeth. Bitter and indignant, Nicholas listened to how commercial interest made compassionate leave impossible.

'Dad, if I let the studio down they say I'll never get work again. We'll come in April, I promise.'

'Are you sure? I hardly like to presume.'

It snowed in the night before Elisabeth's funeral. The vicar and Nicholas led the little group following the coffin; behind them came the housekeeper, Mrs Guthrie, and Parker, the gardener, butler and occasional chauffeur. Cook had left. When they returned from church, Nicholas hid away in the library. Aeschylus, that's what he needed. Aeschylus understood. Over the next three days, he ate just three poached eggs and a Welsh rarebit. Mrs Guthrie feared her catering was inadequate.

'Will you get another cook, sir?'

'No. You know my tastes, Molly, very simple.'

Nicholas passed one afternoon reading in Elisabeth's upstairs room, and discovered that having her things around him made the pain neither better nor worse. She was simply gone, and he was punished with survival. Mrs Guthrie found him talking to his father's portrait on the stairs.

'I wish they'd left me on the beach in Normandy.'

'I beg your pardon, sir?'

'Nothing, nothing.'

He had never needed much company, but now loneliness crushed him. Walking helped. He explored the house he thought he knew and found unfamiliar paths around the estate. In the stable loft he found a little shield and wooden sword, and remembered how when Matthew was eight the two of them had constituted a Roman legion, the Victoria Victrix. Later he came across the rocking horse, still with only one eye, on which six-year-old Matthew had led cavalry at Edgehill. He tipped it with his toe. Perhaps he should telephone the boy. But no, that woman might answer.

Then one day he climbed the narrow stairs to the very top of the house, and stood panting for a minute or two outside Nanny Thompson's old room. A low doorway opposite led into a little room with a window at waist height and a small table and chairs. Bending down, he opened a small chest of drawers and found toddler's clothes smelling slightly of camphor. He picked up a little fleecy pullover, held it to his face, and to his own chagrin started to cry. He shut the drawer and hurried back downstairs.

After supper he steeled himself to telephone California. A female voice answered. It was the childminder; would he like to leave a message.

'No... that is, yes.' He disliked passing messages through a stranger, but shrank from having to make a second call. 'Please say Mr d'Aubigny's father is wondering whether he still intends to visit in the spring.'

When Matthew did not return his call, Nicholas began to worry. What might have happened? An accident? First his mother, then Elisabeth; what if Matthew were dead? For five days the possibility ate into his mind until he would have accepted the worst news as a release from uncertainty. He overheard Mrs Guthrie and Parker talking in the corridor.

'I'm worried about him, George, for his mind, forever patrolling the place like that.'

Parker grunted. The relief when Matthew finally rang left Nicholas almost speechless.

'Hi Dad. Sorry not to call back straight away. It's been bloody here.'

'Ah.'

'I've had a hell of a fire-fight with the studio, a full and frank exchange of views, attorneys, the lot. I think I've won. They want me out, but I got them for breach of contract, and the final settlement's quite juicy.'

'I see.'

'They've given me a Lagonda Rapide as part of it. I knocked them down to ten grand, but it must be worth at least twice that. You know, the pre-war tourer? A yellow one. It was in *The Road to Amalfi.*'

'Ah.'

'Anyway, as soon as things are sorted we're coming home.

'Jolly good.'

'It's been a long time.'

'Yes, ah… four years…'

The old man spent the next few weeks in a state of mounting excitement punctuated with irrational dread that sometimes woke him at night; Matthew in an air crash, Matthew drowning. On the day of their arrival he rose at five. There was nothing to do; all had been prepared. From midday, he kept watch from a second floor window, and eventually spied a yellow speck flickering past distant fields.

'He's coming,' he called to Mrs Guthrie as he hurried down past the kitchen. From the courtyard he could hear the muscular burble of a four-litre engine and watched the splendid tourer approach down the avenue. Hero returning with the spoils of war, he thought. It drew up outside the library and Elaine got out. She was alone. They stared at each other. Neither was prepared for this moment.

'Where's Matthew?' said Nicholas.

'Where indeed?' she replied icily.

Nicholas felt the words like a blow to the chest and stumbled back into the library. At that moment, Mrs Guthrie came down the steps from the front door.

'Are you by yourself, ma'am?'

'We had to hire another car. Matthew's got Dominic and the luggage. They should be here by now. They set off before me and I came the long way round.'

'They'll be here shortly, then. Excuse me, I must just ask Mr d'Aubigny what wine he would like with lunch.'

She went into the library. Elaine heard her call for Parker.

'George, Mr d'Aubigny's fainted.'

But Parker knew better. 'Looks like heart failure. Better get Dr Widdick quick.'

Elaine did not enter the library. There was nothing she could do to help. By the time Mrs Guthrie returned Parker had still grimmer news.

'He don't seem to be breathing, Molly.'

Elaine dug her nails into her palms.

'Not my fault,' she whispered. She lit a cigarette to steady herself, and had just finished it when the second car arrived.

'Where's Dad?' asked Matthew.

'In the library.' She gestured. 'But Matthew…' He turned back to her. 'He's just had a heart attack.'

'Good God! Is he all right?'

'I'm afraid not. I'm terribly sorry… I'm afraid he's dead.'

Little Dominic looked on in wonder as his father fell to his knees on the flagstones and howled.

Inheritance
Sheila Preston

Sixty-five is no age to die. It was thirty years since he had seen Flora. Now the choice to see her again no longer existed.

He walked along an avenue of white flowering cherry trees, their blossom trembling in a gentle breeze. Early for his appointment, he rested on a bench beside the flint backdrop of Norwich Anglican cathedral. He used to sit here as a child.

Most kids who enter the care system do not achieve a university degree. However, as a professor at Columbia University, president of his local synagogue, owning a penthouse in Manhattan, David Stein considered he had overcome the past. And had no one to thank but himself.

When his mother got in touch with David after finding his photograph on Facebook, his reply to her outpouring of regret had been bitter and accusing.

'It was your decision,' he typed. 'You must accept the repercussions.' Who could forgive a mother for putting her child in care? Not him. He would never forgive Flora for the indignity and pain she had caused him. Never.

Of course, Flora kept David's younger brother, Michael – her favourite. He who could do no wrong. It was no surprise when, at the age of nineteen, Michael was diagnosed with schizophrenia. No wonder he was such a pain in the ass when they were kids. Flora wrote she could not cope with two boys who constantly beat hell out of each other. Repeatedly, she came home from work to find the front door glass smashed, or him and Michael down the road pilfering from the supermarket. She begged his father, Irving, to have them, but this idea was vetoed by his new wife.

It took David's father five years to rescue him, and then only for eighteen months during his 'A' Levels. Soon after, Irving fled from London with his next new wife, back to the family business in New York. *We told you not to marry a Shikse*, they jibed, so Irving included in his will a disinheritance clause if either of his sons married a non-Jew. *No more Shikses!* No problem there, thought David. Michael, sabotaging all hope of recovery with alcohol and drugs, was more likely to kill himself than marry. And he himself – overweight and forty – couldn't seem to make it with anyone.

A flurry of white petals from the cherry trees prompted David to look at his watch. He noticed an attractive young woman at the wheel of a Clio, apparently beseeching the assiduous gateman to let her through. David caught the words, 'No need to get upset, Miss,' as the guard wrote a warrant and waved her through. She sped off in the direction of the car park.

She soon reappeared, her blonde hair flying behind her, as she ran over the grass in front of him. She lost one of her high-heeled shoes in the mud. Retracing her steps, she pulled it free, removing her other shoe to race barefoot to the path. Once there, she replaced both shoes and disappeared through the front door of one of the Georgian houses encompassing the cathedral close.

David rose to follow her through the same door, which bore the brass plaque for Letwin Noble, solicitors. After introducing himself at reception, he was led into an elegant waiting room looking onto the cathedral. The blonde was ensconced in one of the sumptuous leather arm chairs, reading the situations vacant supplement of the local newspaper. Her outfit was businesslike: black suit, white blouse. Makeup: immaculate. She smiled at David, revealing a set of perfect teeth. He noticed her look at his tartan trousers before gazing through the window where students of the cathedral school were scurrying between lessons.

Suddenly, the door opened to reveal Mr Letwin, wearing a beige linen suit, accessorised by a rebellious pair of red-framed spectacles hanging from a gold chain around his neck.

'Good morning, Elizabeth.'

Then to David he said, 'Hello, Professor Stein. I'm pleased to meet you. Would you both come this way, please?'

Both. Why both? The blonde sure has a beautiful ass, thought David, following Elizabeth and the solicitor along a corridor punctuated by paintings and photographs of past and present partners of Letwin Noble. Climbing the spiral staircase, Elizabeth's brief skirt revealed bare thighs. David tried not to look.

On the fourth floor they entered a conference room. At the table sat a young man whose suit, David noted, was Armani. His smooth fingers tapered into perfectly manicured nails. They pay these legal guys well, he thought. I hope the price of the suit is not included in his fees. David watched his eyes focus on Elizabeth as she settled on one of the conference chairs. Probably he'd like to whisk her away to Arabia on the back of a white stallion. The Arab rose, nodded at David and extended his hand to Elizabeth. It slipped through her fingers.

Mr Letwin sat at the head of the table, nervously sifting a pile of papers.

'You will be wondering why the three of you are here.' Peering over his spectacles, Mr Letwin continued. 'None of you have met before today, but Elizabeth Sinclair, Dr David Stein and Professor Malek Hoseini, you are all children of Flora de Grey, and you are here for the reading of your mother's will.'

Elizabeth blinked.

'David, of course,' she said. But the Arab? David could read her thoughts. Where did he come from?

David scrutinised the Arab's face. My, Flora certainly got around. A bloody Arab! Who else would be prancing around in an Armani suit in the depths of East Anglia? When and where did Flora dump this child? In Elizabeth's face he recognised his own. Probably relieved to find her two new brothers were at least sane, she beamed from one to the other. But an Arab... how could Flora do such a thing? He could hardly go home and tell everyone he had found a long-lost brother, and by the way, he's a *bone fide* Arab. Take the money and run. Let me out of here.

After a suitable pause, Mr Letwin continued, 'I must leave you to discuss later why your mother didn't arrange for you to meet before she died, while I expedite the reading of the will. Your mother's estate – which is considerable – is to be divided equally into four: Michael's inheritance has been put in a trust, to be managed by the three of you, and in the event of his death divided between you and or any future progeny you might have.

'For you, David, your mother has left a file containing letters and her correspondence with the Social Services, and for you, Malek, a photograph album. It was your mother's wish that the three of you meet to discuss the continuing care of your brother Michael, and how to make appropriate decisions for him throughout the remainder of his life. In her opinion, as a vulnerable adult Michael will never have sufficient mental capacity to manage his inheritance alone and, in order to protect his state benefits, should be given items and sums of money only for specific needs. And...' Mr Letwin briefly looked over his spectacles. 'Not items which will put him in danger or encourage others to take advantage of him. I know your mother particularly hoped you would all share this responsibility equally. Flora has left a letter of wishes in which she states the hope that Elizabeth will reconsider her decision not to go to university.'

Mr Letwin continued with a detailed reading of the will, but no one was listening. Flora's children were readjusting their preconceptions.

When Mr Letwin finished, Malek stood up to kiss his sister on her hand and on both her cheeks. He extended a hand to his brother. David did not move. Mr Letwin finished reading the will and after appropriate pleasantries led them back down the stairs.

'I know where we can talk,' said Elizabeth and led her brothers to a nearby bistro. Over coffee, they sat and looked at each other.

'I knew nothing of our mother's existence until two weeks after she died,' Malek explained. 'I grew up in Algeria with my father Aba Zuz and my mother Nourradine. My father met Flora in the 1980s when writing his Ph.D. in Nuclear Physics at Sheffield University.'

David interrupted: 'When we left Sheffield, I remember saying goodbye to your father. We dropped him off at the university. I can see him now. He was crying.' David paused as if searching his memory.

'Michael and I spent that summer with our grandmother. It must have been when you were born. I had no idea.'

Malek continued, 'My father told me that your grandmother never forgave Flora for the divorce. She wouldn't help Flora. Your father's new wife didn't want you. Your mother really struggled. It would never happen in an Arab family.' He bit his lip. 'My father convinced her to go home with him to give birth. My grandmother, Farida, delivered me and cared for me after Flora went home. My father understood. She had to return to look after you and Michael. After his military service, my father married Nourradine, my mother. They said it was the will of Allah that Flora left me. They were blessed with no other children.'

'How sad.' Elizabeth touched the top of Malek's hand.

'Flora and Aba Zuz corresponded regularly. With the blessing of Allah, our mother prospered and even though we did not need it, Flora sent money regularly for my education. Aba Zus loved our mother very much and says he always will.'

David said, 'She never mentioned you, Malek. But like you, I have not spoken to our mother for over thirty years. Did you know about Malek, Elizabeth?'

'No.'

'So we have something in common, brother', said Malek. 'My father always said our mother would have made a good Muslim. She used to tell him her Jewish family were exactly the same as the Arabs: full of passion and love. He wasn't surprised when she married a holy man from her own culture. Living in a culture different from the one you are born in is hard. In the end, our mother decided she needed to regain her own.'

71

Malek touched Elizabeth's hand.

'And what do you do, sister?'

'I work for a local insurance company. I do death claims. Stressful stuff. My father was a dean, here at the cathedral. Consequently, I was offered a sixth-form scholarship. Mother was devastated when I left school early. She never said it. But I know how she felt. My friends are now returning to Norwich with degrees, going off on gap years to exotic places like China. I'm sorry now that I didn't take that place. Maybe I can retrace my steps. Will you help me?'

'Of course,' David replied. 'Do you have a boyfriend?'

'Yes, he's a mushroom picker. Dad died when I was five. He left Mum only three thousand pounds. With that as the deposit on her first house, she started the property company.

'Life was very difficult with Michael being ill. I spent days with Mother at the mental hospital when Michael had crises. Every time he came out, it took ages to rehabilitate him. His needs always came first. He's stable now and knows his limitations. Sad to say, his life is desperately lonely. He will be delighted to meet you, Malek, and see David again. He is a lovely person and one of the kindest people I know.'

'I'm looking forward to meeting him,' said Malek. 'David, my father was horrified when Flora gave you to the authorities. My father said you were very difficult boys. Your father should have taken you. Flora fought for years to get you back.

'I want you to know that I was not brought up with the prejudices of my fellow Palestinians. We Arabs are Semites just like you Jews: made from the same flesh and blood. After 9/11, studying for my doctorate in the States, I got used to mistrust and fear. I used to pass myself off as French. Most of my professors were Jewish and to them I owe my present success and reputation.

'My father told me that after living in three different cultures, Flora belonged not to one alone, but all of them. She lost three of her children – even Michael – to madness. We do not know what she went through. Sometimes the right decision is not available. Our mother did what she thought was best for all of us. And now we must do the best for each other.'

'I like your suit, Malek,' said David.

'I bought it in Palermo. I go there often for mathematics conferences. Give me your measurements and I'll get you one.'

'Shall we meet tomorrow at mother's?' suggested Elizabeth.

'That's a good idea,' said David. 'And maybe we could visit Michael.' Both Malek and Elizabeth nodded.

That night, David read through the file of letters given to him by the solicitor. There was an envelope containing letters written in his childlike hand to his mother. They were filed in date order.

At the beginning of his time in care he wrote: *Dear Mummy, It was lovely to see you today and I can't wait to see you again.* As time went on the letters became haunted.

What the Social Services or S.S. for short are looking at is for you to be more consistent. They write everything down on paper. Where you live. What you do. Everything. They have spies everywhere. If you want to get me back Tony and Margaret – David winced at the memory of his foster parents – *must see **consistency**. Then they will be more allies to you than enemies.*

And later: *I decided that because we haven't lived together for so long the risk is too great. Margaret and John say that if I come home to you, I might end up in a children's home and lose everything I have tried to establish here.*

And finally: *My social worker told me that you sent him a letter regarding our contact. You must have read a copy of the review. I clearly stated that for everybody's sake I do not wish to see you for the foreseeable future: that being at such a time when I am grown up and no longer in care.*

He could not remember writing these letters. The word 'consistency' stuck in his gut.

There were other letters in the file, obtained twenty years later under the Freedom of Information Act – notes on reviews with large areas blanked out, all indicating how the S.S. and his foster parents had connived to prevent Flora from seeing him.

David wept.

On the way to meet his siblings the next day, the Jewish saying heard so often: 'My brother, the doctor... the lawyer... the brain surgeon...' took on a new meaning for David. A bit unusual, true, but he hoped he could now say, 'My brother, the Arab...' and be proud of it.